MW00654006

DARING DEVOTION

A 31-DAY JOURNEY

WITH THOSE WHO LIVED

GOD'S PROMISES

M. R. CONRAD

CHURCH
WORKS
WWW.CHURCHWORKSMEDIA.COM

©2020 All Rights Reserved.

Daring Devotion: A 31-Day Journey with Those Who Lived God's Promises
Copyright ©2020 by M. R. Conrad
All rights reserved. This book or parts thereof may not be reproduced in any form, stored in any
retrieval system, or transmitted in any form by any means—electronic, mechanical, photocopy,
recording, or otherwise—without prior written permission of the publisher, except as provided
by United States of America copyright law. For permission requests, write to
connect@churchworksmedia.com.

Scripture references are from the King James Version.

Published by Church Works Media
FIRST EDITION 2020
Editing by Ivan Mesa, Joe Tyrpak, and Chris Anderson
Cover design, illustrations, and layout by Erik Peterson with Joe Tyrpak

ISBN 978-1-7343978-2-6 (paperback)
www.mrconrad.net
www.churchworksmedia.com

TABLE OF CONTENTS

CHRONOLOGICAL
TABLE OF CONTENTS

MAP OF WHERE
GOD'S PROMISES LED

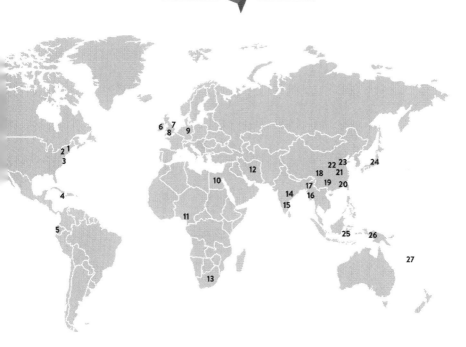

1 David Brainerd	15 Amy Carmichael
2 John Eliot	16 Adoniram Judson
3 Edward Judson	17 Sarah Hall Boardman Judson
4 George Liele	18 Isobel Kuhn
5 Jim & Elisabeth Elliot	19 James Fraser
6 Patrick of Ireland	20 Robert Morrison
7 George Müller	21 J. Hudson Taylor
8 William Tyndale	22 Eric Liddell
9 Nicholas Ludwig von Zinzendorf	23 John and Betty Stam
10 William Borden	24 Stephen Metcalf
11 Mary Slessor	25 Darlene Deibler Rose
12 Henry Martyn	26 Stanley Dale
13 David Livingstone	27 John Paton
14 William Carey	

CHART OF INFLUENCE

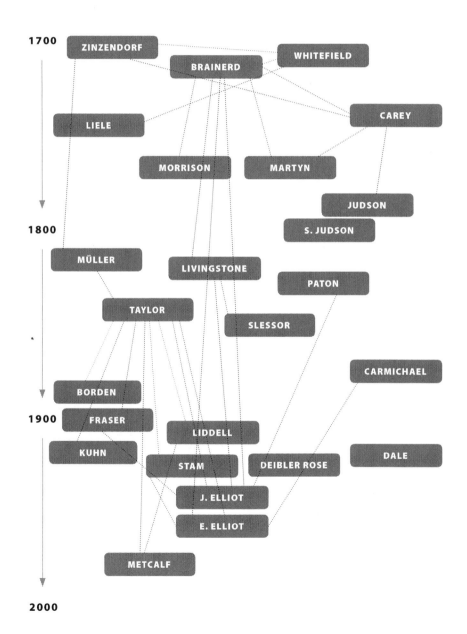

1700

ZINZENDORF
BRAINERD
WHITEFIELD
LIELE
CAREY
MORRISON
MARTYN
JUDSON

1800

S. JUDSON
MÜLLER
LIVINGSTONE
PATON
TAYLOR
SLESSOR
CARMICHAEL
BORDEN

1900

FRASER
LIDDELL
KUHN
DALE
STAM
DEIBLER ROSE
J. ELLIOT
E. ELLIOT
METCALF

2000

PREFACE

JOURNEY BRIEFING

*"And what shall I more say? for the time would fail me to tell
of Gideon, and of Barak, and of Samson, and of Jephthae; of
David also, and Samuel, and of the prophets: Who through
faith subdued kingdoms, wrought righteousness, obtained
promises, stopped the mouths of lions, Quenched the violence
of fire, escaped the edge of the sword, out of weakness were
made strong, waxed valiant in fight, turned to flight the armies
of the aliens. Women received their dead raised to life again:
and others were tortured, not accepting deliverance; that they
might obtain a better resurrection: And others had trial of
cruel mockings and scourgings, yea, moreover of bonds and
imprisonment: They were stoned, they were sawn asunder, were
tempted, were slain with the sword: they wandered about in
sheepskins and goatskins; being destitute, afflicted, tormented;
Of whom the world was not worthy."*

—HEBREWS 11:32–38

I invite you to read this book as an uninspired extension of
Hebrews 11 into the twenty-first century. Hebrews 11, often
called the "Hall of Faith," provides brief glimpses into the lives of

those who acted on the promises of God. The writer of Hebrews does not give their whole biographies. He does not endorse every action, decision, speech, or belief of these men and women. Instead, the inspired author highlights how each one acted on the promises of God.

God knows we as Christians not only require propositional truth but also incarnated truth. We need to see biblical principles and promises lived out by common people throughout history and in diverse cultures. A. W. Tozer wrote, "Next to the Holy Scriptures the greatest aid to the life of faith may be Christian biography."[1] Jonathan Edwards agrees: "There are two ways of representing and recommending true religion and virtue to the world; the one, by doctrine and precept; the other, by instance and example; both are abundantly used in the Holy Scriptures."[2]

I have found this to be true in my life. The Lord used many of the biographies referenced in this devotional to disciple me as a young man considering God's will for my life. These books compelled me to do what few around me dared to try. If God could use the weak, flawed men and women of these biographies because they trusted God's promises, could He not do the same with me?

Others through history report similar experiences. William Carey, after reading accounts of the lives of David Brainerd and John Eliot, points to them as models for his own life and work. Henry Martyn's journals speak of the influence of David Brainerd and William Carey. Jim Elliot, Isobel Kuhn, and many others testify of spiritual growth cultivated through reading Mrs. Howard Taylor's two-volume biography of Hudson Taylor. Elisabeth Elliot, who knew Amy Carmichael only through her writings, calls her "my first spiritual mother" who "showed me the shape of godliness."[3] The testimonies of those who lived God's promises attract and inspire those surrendered to God to also live "by every word that proceedeth out of the mouth of God" (Matthew 4:4).

I designed *Daring Devotion* to be a gateway to a wealth of spiritual encouragement. May this book give this generation a taste of what God and His promises have meant to faithful men and women who ran the race before us. May God awaken a hunger within you to learn more of these devoted servants—to read their biographies and see how God worked in their lives. Having feasted on God's faithfulness to those of the past, may you be inspired to step out on the promises of God and take godly risks for His sake.

Be careful as you read this book. It may compel you into a life of deeper dedication to God. Elisabeth Elliot wrote of the risk of reading her husband's story, and her warning applies to all biographies of godly people:

> Let this be a warning. You can't be too careful what you read. This man's story might do three things: (1) Give you someone to imitate—not a model of perfection by any means, but a man of "like passions" with the rest of us, whose heart was set on God. (2) Show you a pattern of God's sovereign love in the twenty-eight years of a real flesh-and-blood man of our century. (3) Demonstrate that obedience is costly, but the rewards of obedience are priceless—among the few things we *cannot* lose.[4]

The examples in this book may inspire you to step out for God in a way you have never before considered.

This book contains thirty-one readings—one for each day of a month. My hope is that you will use this to supplement your personal devotional time. This book is no substitute for the Word of God. I suggest that you continue opening your day with God as you normally do. Add this book afterward. Better yet, establish a second time with God in the evening, and use this book as a guide.

I have arranged each chapter in a topical manner. However, if you would prefer to read chronologically, please refer to the chronological table of contents. I have also included a map showing how those who lived God's promises spread across the world. Additionally, there is a chart that begins to show how Christian biographies have influenced others to follow Christ.

We know of the lives of these men and women because they or others recorded their stories. They represent the unnamed thousands who have served faithfully throughout the centuries. Those highlighted here are a mere sampling of those who lived God's promises.

Like those listed by God in Hebrews 11, these men and women, though champions of the gospel and faithful in their service, were flawed. As we read their writings, we find that they were often aware of and humbled by their failings. From our contemporary perspective, we may also be shocked by areas of their lives in which we perceive them to be blinded by their upbringing, times, and culture.

Writing in the late nineteenth century, J. C. Ryle, in the foreword of his brief biography of George Whitefield, cautions on how we should view Christians of the past:

> The story of Whitefield's times is one that should often be told. Without it, no body is qualified to form an opinion either as to the man or his acts. Conduct that in one kind of times may seem rash, extravagant, and indiscreet, in another may be wise, prudent, and even absolutely necessary. In forming your opinion of the compara-

tive merits of Christian men, never forget the old rule: "Distinguish between times." Place yourself in each man's position. Do not judge what was a right course of action in other times, by what seems a right course of action in your own.[5]

In the future, people will look back at us. They will see areas in which we have erred or been blinded by our times. Future generations of believers may have caveats about our lives and ministries. I pray they also will say we were faithful to God and the gospel of Jesus Christ. May we extend to those before us the grace that we ourselves wish to receive from those who follow us.

THE STARTING POINT

The story of each of the people highlighted in this book begins at the same place—the gospel of Jesus Christ. Long before these men and women lived the promises of God, they first believed the gospel, God's greatest promise of all. The transforming work of the gospel ignited their daring devotion to the cause of Christ.

"Dead! Lost! Lost!"[1] The words echoed in twenty-year-old Adoniram Judson's head as he stumbled out of the inn. He had entered the night before as a confident intellectual. Judson, the 1807 valedictorian of Brown University, had thrown off the shackles of his father's religion for the freedom of his classmate Jacob Eames' atheism. One night changed everything. One night showed Judson his own true spiritual condition before God, a condition common to all of humanity.

"I am very sorry," the innkeeper had said the day before as Judson checked into the hotel. "The only room I have left is beside a critically ill gentleman." Judson assured the innkeeper that this would be no problem. However, as the night wore on, the muted groans from next door made sleep impossible and set

Judson's mind to contemplating his own mortality. Was the sick man next door ready for death? Was he himself prepared to leave this world? By morning, Judson had banished those thoughts from his mind. What would Jacob Eames and his other intellectual peers at Brown think of him if they knew his doubts?

As Judson paid his bill, he inquired about the man in the next room.

"He's dead," said the innkeeper. "The poor man died in the night."

"What was his name?" asked Judson.

"Jacob Eames."

"Dead! Lost! Lost!" These words which haunted Judson as he learned of his friend's death reflect truths he learned as a child. The Bible uses these terms—*dead* and *lost*—to describe the spiritual condition of every person on earth. Each person is "dead in trespasses and sins" (Ephesians 2:1). God declares that "the wages of sin is death" (Romans 6:23) and that "your iniquities have separated between you and your God, and your sins have hid his face from you" (Isaiah 59:2). Since the sin of the first man and woman God created, every person has been a sinner by birth and by choice. Isaiah wrote, "All we like sheep have gone astray; we have turned every one to his own way" (Isaiah 53:6). Everyone has crossed God's line, broken God's law, and missed God's holy mark. Left to ourselves, none of us can escape God's just judgment of eternity in hell. Everyone needs a Savior, and that is exactly what God promised in the gospel.

At Jesus Christ's birth, the angels announced, "For unto you is born this day . . . a Savior, which is Christ the Lord" (Luke 2:11). The four Gospels of the New Testament unmistakably reveal that this Savior is God in human form. Jesus did what only God could do, miraculously healing the sick, raising the dead, and even forgiving sins. Furthermore, He claimed to be God, clearly stating, "I and my Father are one" (John 10:30). Throughout His ministry, Jesus proclaimed His reason for coming to earth: "For the Son of man is come to seek and to save that which was lost" (Luke 19:10).

In saving the lost, Jesus dared to lay down His own life. In a move that stunned followers and enemies alike, Jesus willingly submitted to the indignity and torture of the cross, bearing the punishment that sinners deserve. He died that we might live. First Peter 3:18 explains: "For Christ also hath once suffered for sins, the just [sinless Jesus] for the unjust [every sinner in the world], that he might bring us to God." Only the death of the perfect Son of God could reconcile sinners sentenced to eternal separation from God.

The shock of Jesus' death was surpassed only by the impossibility of what happened three days later: Jesus came back to life! Yet, Jesus had already proclaimed He would rise again, stating before His death, "I lay down my life, that I might take it again" (John 10:17). Only God could do this. In amazement, Jesus' followers stared at the nail prints in His hands. The apostle Thomas said what they all were thinking: "My Lord and my God!" (John 20:28). They believed the gospel.

What is the gospel? Paul described it in 1 Corinthians 15:1–4: "I declare unto you the gospel . . . how that Christ died for our sins according to the scriptures; And that he was buried, and that he rose again the third day according to the scriptures." The gospel—the good news of Jesus' death and resurrection for the salvation of humanity—fulfilled God's promise of sending a Savior to rescue those lost in sin.

How does the gospel save sinners? God's Word repeatedly emphasizes that we are saved by faith in Jesus Christ. Jesus Himself said, "He that believeth on the Son hath everlasting life: and he that believeth not the Son shall not see life; but the wrath of God abideth on him" (John 3:36). Romans 10:9 states, "If thou shalt confess with thy mouth the Lord Jesus, and shalt believe in thine heart that God hath raised him from the dead, thou shalt be saved." Ephesians 2:8–9 clarifies that the gospel saves apart from our good works: "For by grace are ye saved through faith; and that not of yourselves: it is the gift of God: Not of works, lest any man should boast." Again, Titus 3:5 proclaims, "Not by works of righteousness which we have done, but according to his mercy he saved us." The gospel requires no work to earn salvation. Rather, it forbids any attempt to add to what Christ has already done to save us. A sinner must repent, turning from his own way and works, and trust Christ alone.

Each of the men and women highlighted in this book started their spiritual life by repenting of their sin and placing their faith in Christ's death and resurrection. They believed the gospel. Have you believed the gospel?

The gospel that saves also inspires those who believe to obey Christ's commands. During the forty days following His resurrection, Jesus repeatedly emphasized one specific command— an imperative known today as the Great Commission. Each of the Gospels and the book of Acts records this commission. The Gospel of Mark is most succinct: "Go ye into all the world, and preach the gospel to every creature" (Mark 16:15).

From the apostles in the first century until today, faithful believers have risked their lives to obey the Great Commission. Like the apostle Paul, they concluded that if Christ dared to *die* for them, they must *live* for Him. Paul testified, "For the love of Christ constraineth us; because we thus judge, that if one died for all, then were all dead: And that he died for all, that they which live should not henceforth live unto themselves, but unto him which died for them, and rose again" (2 Corinthians 5:14–15). For some, living for Christ included dying for Him. For all the people highlighted in this book, living for Christ meant a reordering of priorities and life goals for the glory of God and the furthering of His work in the world.

The gospel changed Adoniram Judson's life in precisely this way. After that sleepless night in the hotel listening to his friend's dying groans, he responded to the convicting work of the Holy Spirit and trusted Christ as his Savior. From that point, the trajectory of his life changed completely. Adoniram Judson—the intellectual skeptic transformed by the gospel—not only started a new life in Christ but also eventually became the first American to be sent abroad as a foreign missionary. Without the gospel's life-changing power, Judson would never have risked his life to take the message of Jesus Christ to the jungles of Burma (modern-day Myanmar).

The gospel is the starting point. In every account in this book, God's greatest promise became the foundation for lives built upon the promises of God in His Word. The gospel that sparked their daring devotion continues to compel God's people today to live and die for Christ.

DAY 1

---◂---

WEAK GIANTS

"All God's giants have been weak men who did great things for God because they reckoned on His being with them."

—J. HUDSON TAYLOR, MISSIONARY TO CHINA (1832–1905)

"But God hath chosen the foolish things of the world to confound the wise; and God hath chosen the weak things of the world to confound the things which are mighty; And base things of the world, and things which are despised, hath God chosen, yea, and things which are not, to bring to nought things that are: That no flesh should glory in his presence."

—1 CORINTHIANS 1:27–29

Though the Civil War in America ended months before, another battle raged across the Atlantic in the heart of thirty-three-year-old Hudson Taylor. *What more could be done to reach the millions in China with the gospel?* This burden drove Taylor from a worship service full of joyful believers to pacing and praying on a lonely beach in Brighton, England.

Taylor had labored in China for over six years until his health broke. Doctors warned him that if he did not return to England,

DARING DEVOTION

he would almost certainly die. Now, nearly six years exiled in England from his mission field, Taylor labored for China from afar. Even before his recovery, Taylor filled his hours with Chinese translation work. He accepted speaking engagements across the United Kingdom to publicize the spiritual needs of China. If the Lord spared his life, Taylor planned to return to China, but he did not want to return alone.

As the tide played at his feet, Taylor struggled with the weight of taking responsibility for those who would go with him to China. How could he call young men and women to leave the safety of England for a life of danger on the other side of the world? Taylor himself barely survived his first attempt. He keenly understood the risk. Faithful people would answer the call, never to return to their families in England. How could he shoulder so great a responsibility?

Taylor found the answer in the promises of God. He asked himself, "If God gives us a band of men for inland China, and they go, and all die of starvation even, they will only be taken straight to heaven; and if one heathen soul is saved, would it not be well worth while?"[1] This most basic promise, the promise of eternal life, spurred Taylor to action.

That morning of June 25, 1865, Taylor prayed for God to call twenty-four new workers to accompany him to China. God would answer his prayer. These twenty-four would become the first of hundreds to serve under the China Inland Mission.

We think of people like Hudson Taylor or the list of men and women in Hebrews 11 as heroes of the faith—people with talents, abilities, and strength far beyond our own. However, when God is looking for people to use, He is not looking for heroes. God is the hero of His story and the central figure in every biography of those He uses in His work.

The men and women chronicled in Hebrews 11 "out of weakness were made strong" (Hebrews 11:24). They are not listed for their heroic abilities but for their faith. Why did they need faith? Because their strength was not enough, and they knew it. Like us, they had weakness and faults, but they looked to the One who has no weaknesses or faults. They trusted God and His promises, not their own strength.

Hudson Taylor was no stranger to weakness. At age eleven, his frequent illnesses kept him from attending school for months at a time. During his medical studies, he survived exposure to a deadly disease. When he lived in China, illness often brought his ministry to a standstill, forcing him to convalescent retreats.

Reminders of his weakness would continue beyond that fateful morning on Brighton Beach. The next year, Taylor returned to China. Despite his training as a medical doctor, he would watch his wife die of tuberculosis four years later at the age of thirty-three. Of his eight children, only four would pass the age of ten. Of his own condition, he wrote,

> [I am] often sick in body, as well as perplexed in mind and embarrassed by circumstances; had not the Lord been specially gracious to me, had not my mind been sustained by the conviction that the work is His, and that He is with me in what it is no empty figure to call "the thick of the conflict," I must have fainted and broken down.[2]

In 1870, a liver disease plagued him, robbing him of sleep and leading to recurring bouts of depression.

Through Taylor's weakness, God continued to work. Mrs. Howard Taylor, his biographer and daughter-in-law, wrote,

It was not until many years later, when Mr. Taylor could look back over all the way in which the Lord had led him, that he was impressed with the fact that every important advance in the development of the Mission had sprung from or been directly connected with times of sickness or suffering which had cast him in a special way upon God.[3]

In November of 1875, forty-three-year-old Taylor wrote,

How many estimate difficulties in the light of their own resources, and thus attempt little and often fail in the little they attempt! All God's giants have been weak men, who did great things for God because they reckoned on His being with them.[4]

Taylor's words echo the truths of 1 Corinthians 1:27–29:

But God hath chosen the foolish things of the world to confound the wise; and God hath chosen the weak things of the world to confound the things which are mighty; And base things of the world, and things which are despised, hath God chosen, yea, and things which are not, to bring to nought things that are: That no flesh should glory in his presence.

Taylor was weak enough for God to use him to bring thousands to Christ and into God's work in the most populous nation in the world.

PERSONAL REFLECTION

- What is the greatest obstacle for God to use me?
  Is it my pride?

- What weakness is holding me back that could instead be the
  avenue of God's power through me?

- What excuses am I making for disobedience because of
  factors God has sovereignly placed in my life? Could God not
  transform these weaknesses into obvious expressions of His
  power?

- If God were to use me in a great way, would He or I
  get the glory?

FURTHER READING   **1 Corinthians 1:18–31**

Taylor, Dr. & Mrs. Howard. *Hudson Taylor in Early Years: The
Growth of a Soul.* Singapore: OMF International, 1911.

Taylor, Dr. & Mrs. Howard. *Hudson Taylor and the China
Inland Mission: The Growth of a Work of God.* Singapore: OMF
International, 1918.

DAY 2

———— ◄ ————

SUFFICIENT GRACE

"But my child, my grace is sufficient for thee. Not was or shall be, but it is sufficient."

—DARLENE DEIBLER ROSE,

MISSIONARY TO INDONESIA (1917–2004)

"And he said unto me, My grace is sufficient for thee: for my strength is made perfect in weakness. Most gladly therefore will I rather glory in my infirmities, that the power of Christ may rest upon me."

—2 CORINTHIANS 12:9

Lord, I'd go anywhere for You, no matter what it cost!" said ten-year-old Darlene MacIntosh in rural Iowa.[1] Ten years later, in 1938, Darlene Deibler and her husband of one year disembarked for the first time in Indonesia. The cost of following Christ would surpass anything she could have imagined.

The sacrifices of the next three years met Darlene's expectations. As pioneer missionaries, she and her husband, Russell Deibler, braved the jungles of Papua, Indonesia, taking the gospel to remote tribes for the first time. Unknown to them at the time, the struggle to survive in this environment caused permanent damage to her husband's heart. However, they saw souls saved and God at work.

Then World War II struck. The Japanese conquered Indonesia. The invaders interned all foreign nationals in work camps. On Friday, March 13, 1942, the Japanese separated Darlene from her husband. As he stood in the back of an open truck, Russell whispered down to her, "Remember one thing, dear: God said that He would never leave us nor forsake us."[2] The words of this promise from Hebrews 13:5 were the last Darlene would ever hear from her husband's lips.

Russell would die a year later of dysentery and complications from an undiagnosed heart condition in the men's work camp in Pare Pare, Indonesia. When Darlene's captors informed her of her husband's passing, the promises of God's Word assuaged the feelings of abandonment that flooded her soul. The words of Isaiah 43:2 comforted her: "My child, did I not say that when thou passest through the waters I would be with thee, and through the floods, they would not overflow thee?"[3]

Darlene Deibler clung to God's promises. Verses memorized as a child braced her to face each day's trials. Over her three years in the Japanese internment camp, Darlene daily endured forced labor, dietary deprivations, psychological tortures, untreated diseases, battles with vermin, and other personal indignities. She suffered with her friends, wept as they lost loved ones, and watched in distress as fellow prisoners and former coworkers broke down mentally under the strain. Among all these trials, Darlene ministered to her fellow prisoners, sharing with them the promises that kept her going. She even dared to share the gospel with the violent Japanese officer in charge of the work camp.

At her darkest hour as a prisoner of the Japanese secret police, Darlene sat alone in solitary confinement on death row. Emotionally spent from hours of interrogation and wondering if her accusers truly believed her to be an American spy, Darlene yielded to torrents of tears which soaked her filthy dress. At that moment, the words of 2 Corinthians 12:9 comforted her. She later wrote, "When there were no more tears to cry, I would hear Him whisper, 'But my child, my grace is sufficient for thee. Not was nor shall be, but it is sufficient.' Oh, the eternal, ever-present, undiminished supply of God's glorious grace."[4] That grace came not only in the form of comfort but also as answers to her prayers. God's miraculous grace delivered her when she should have died, healed her when medicine was not available, and even turned enemies into allies. At times, God showed unexpected kindnesses, like when Darlene prayed for one nutritious banana in solitary confinement and received ninety-two!

She would write, quoting Hebrews 11:1, "Evidence not seen—that was what I put my trust in—not in feelings or moments of ecstasy, but in the unchanging person of Christ."[5] Referencing 2 Corinthians 1:10, she knew Christ to be the One "Who delivered . . . and doth deliver . . . He will yet deliver."[6] Darlene Deibler lived the promises of the God she loved and served.

What did it cost Darlene Deibler to follow Christ? Her husband, her coworkers, her friends, her freedom, her security, her health, her treasured wedding gifts, and all her earthly possessions. When she was finally freed at the end of the war, the only thing she owned was the dress she wore out of the prison gates. Despite her losses, Darlene later testified, "If I could change anything of my life . . . I don't know of anything that I would want changed."[7]

God's grace is sufficient. God's promises, even in the darkest hour, prove true. We can look at the faith of this young woman and through her see the faithfulness of our God.

PERSONAL REFLECTION

- In what ways am I discontent with what God has graciously allowed in my life?

- How can I find God's grace sufficient in difficult circumstances when others would only see deficiencies?

- If I lost everything, how could I prevent bitterness from blinding me to God's grace?

- Have I memorized enough of God's promises that, if I were to be deprived of my Bible, I could still rest on the promises of God?

FURTHER READING   **2 Corinthians 12:1–10**

Rose, Darlene Deibler. *Evidence Not Seen: A Woman's Miraculous Faith in the Jungles of World War II.* San Francisco: Harper & Row, 1988.

DAY 3

---◀---

AS BRIGHT AS THE PROMISES OF GOD

"[The prospects are] as bright as the promises of God."
—ADONIRAM JUDSON, MISSIONARY TO BURMA (1788–1850)

"He staggered not at the promise of God through unbelief;
but was strong in faith, giving glory to God;
And being fully persuaded that, what he had promised,
he was able also to perform."
—ROMANS 4:20–21

Death prison. The name struck fear into Burmese and foreigner alike. Many who entered never returned, and those who returned were never the same again. Dragged by ropes bound around his wrists, thirty-five-year-old Adoniram Judson stumbled through the mud at the gates of the prison.

Despite nearly ten years of peaceful ministry in Burma, the war that began in 1823 between Britain and Burma sealed Judson's fate. On June 8, 1824, officials rounded up the foreigners—whether British, American, or even Greek—and dragged them to the death prison. To oversee the prison, the government employed Spotted Faces, their branded cheeks attesting to their violent crimes. The leader, marked for murder, demanded that the political prisoners call him father. He delighted in torturing "his children."

Besides Judson's own physical distress, he had many other reasons to fret. Nancy, his pregnant wife, lived unprotected not far from the prison. Corrupt government officials frequently visited to steal their belongings and harass her. The few believers from their fledgling work faced grave danger because of their association with the foreigners. Furthermore, Judson's incomplete Burmese translation of the Bible, the fruit of years of labor, faced imminent destruction.

Not long after Judson's detention, Nancy brought the translation manuscript to the death prison. Both Judson and his wife feared that those who often searched their home would steal or destroy it. At first, Nancy had buried the documents, but she knew that months underground in the damp earth of the tropical climate would disintegrate the frail papers. To keep the manuscript from being confiscated by the prison guards, Nancy sewed it into a filthy pillow. When she brought it to her husband, none of the Spotted Faces had any interest in a disgusting pillow as hard as a rock! Every night, Adoniram slept on his life's work.[1]

After eleven months in death prison, the king ordered Judson and the rest of the prisoners to be moved further into the jungle. The Spotted Faces mustered them out so quickly that none of their few possessions accompanied them, including Judson's rock-hard pillow. While Nancy ran to the palace to demand news of her husband, a faithful, Burmese believer, Maung Ing, gave up

· his teacher for dead and scoured the abandoned prison for any memento of his mentor.

Throughout his life, Adoniram Judson understood the menace of darkness in this world. Before his salvation, he had embraced atheism and had witnessed his friend's hopeless death in its grasp. As a young missionary, Judson had assaulted the long-entrenched dominion of Satan in Burma where for countless generations darkness blinded the eyes and deadened the soul in pagan rites. In war, the utter depravity of humankind reared its ugly head. For over a year, he experienced forced deprivations and torture while witnessing wanton cruelty to his fellow prisoners. Disease robbed him of his first two wives and his first three children. Dark times of despair afflicted his soul. Yet, he could look ahead in hope. The darkness would not win over the light. Years later in Boston, when asked about the prospects of his work against such odds, Judson answered, "[The prospects are] as bright as the promises of God."[2]

God always keeps His word, and in the case of Judson, God literally kept His Word. When the war ended in late 1825, Maung Ing delivered the lost Burmese translation to Judson. This faithful believer had providentially discovered it months before while searching the abandoned death camp for a personal memento. God had preserved both the translator and the translation through the war.

Not long after his release, Judson began to see a harvest. During the nine years in Burma before his imprisonment, only eighteen Burmese had come to Christ. In the five years afterward, the number of believers rose to 373.[3] Judson continued work on the Burmese Bible, completing it in 1834.

When all earthly hope fades, the promises of God shine through. We live "in hope of eternal life, which God, that cannot lie, promised before the world began" (Titus 1:2). The Word of God declares, "God is not a man, that he should lie; neither the son of man, that he should repent: hath he said, and shall he not do it? or hath he spoken, and shall he not make it good?" (Numbers 23:19). God's character guarantees He will always keep His promises.

PERSONAL REFLECTION

- To what specific promises do I cling when life whirls out of control?
- On what do I base my hope for the future?
- On what aspects of God's character can I depend when discouragement threatens to swallow up my confidence in God?

FURTHER READING **Romans 4:13–25**

Anderson, Courtney. *To the Golden Shore: The Life of Adoniram Judson.* Valley Forge, PA: Judson Press, 1987.

IMMORTAL TILL MY WORK WAS DONE

"Looking up in unceasing prayer to our dear Lord Jesus, I left all in His hands, and felt immortal till my work was done." [1]

—JOHN PATON, MISSIONARY TO VANUATU (1824–1907)

"Lo, I am with you alway, even unto the end of the world. Amen."

—MATTHEW 28:20

John Paton died an old man in his own bed. For most, this would not be remarkable. For a missionary to cannibals, Paton's longevity was the miraculous work of God.

When Paton left Scotland in 1858 to take the gospel to the South Pacific islands of Vanuatu (then called New Hebrides), he immediately began testing the Lord's promise in Matthew 28:20. When Christ said, "Lo, I am with you alway, even unto the end of the world," did our Lord mean He would be with someone who purposely moved to an island of cannibals? Did He mean His presence would sustain His people in an age ravaged by epidemics? Could Christ's presence combat the constant mental strain of living on a knife's edge of imminent peril? As Paton wrote,

> With regard to my life amongst the Cannibals, as I had only once to die, I was content to leave the time and place and means in the hand of God who had already marvelously preserved me when visiting cholera patients and the fever-stricken poor [in the U.K. prior to his work in Vanuatu]; on that score I had positively no further concern, having left it all absolutely to the Lord, whom I sought to serve and honor, whether in life or by death.[2]

Was such a pronouncement recklessness or profound faith in the promises of God? Paton believed he was simply taking Christ at His Word. As he reflected,

> Without that abiding consciousness of the presence and power of my dear Lord and Saviour, nothing else in all the world could have preserved me from losing my reason and perishing miserably. His words, "Lo, I am with you alway, even unto the end of the world," came to me so real that it would not have startled me to behold Him, as Stephen did, gazing down upon the scene. I felt His supporting power, as did St. Paul, when he cried, "I can do all things through Christ which strengthened me." It is the sober truth, and it comes back to me sweetly after twenty years, that I had my nearest and dearest glimpses of the face and smile of my blessed Lord in those dread moments when musket, club, or spear was being leveled at my life. Oh the bliss of living and enduring, as seeing "Him who is invisible!"[3]

Such was Paton's consistent testimony. He wrote, "This is strength;—this is peace:—to feel, in entering on every day, that all its duties and trials have been committed to the Lord Jesus,— that, come what may, He will use us for His glory and our own real good!"[4]

In 1862, during what might be considered the most dangerous episode of his life, John Paton's survival hung in the balance. Caught in tribal warfare escalated by European traders and the muskets they sold to the warring clans, Paton tried to protect his life and the lives of those who had turned to Christ during his first five years in Vanuatu. He urged Christian and non-Christian alike to fear God. A couple of chieftains challenged his claims.

"'Who fears Jehovah?' [asked one chief] 'He was not here to protect you to-day!' 'Yes,' [Paton] said, 'My Jehovah God is here now. He hears all we say, sees all we do, and will punish the wicked and protect His own people.'"[5]

His enemies did not believe his words, and Paton fled for his life to a neighboring village. The treacherous chief Miaki, who had for a time pretended to be his friend, dispatched warriors to kill him. Chief Nowar, the leader of the village to which Paton had fled for refuge, promised to protect him. However, when he saw the coming warriors, Nowar refused to let the missionary stay in the safety of the chief's house.

"Run into my plantation and climb the tall chestnut tree," Nowar said. "We will bring word when it is safe."

With no other choice, Paton spent the night in the tree. Gunfire and shouts below broke the stillness of the jungle. He had no certainty that those currently claiming to be his protectors would not turn out to be his betrayers.

He would later testify of that night:

Alone, yet not alone! If it be to glorify my God, I will not grudge to spend many nights alone in such a tree, to feel again my Saviour's spiritual presence, to enjoy His consoling fellowship. If thus thrown back upon your own soul, alone, all, all alone, in the midnight, in the bush, in the very embrace of death itself, have you a Friend that will not fail you then?[6]

We, too, can claim the promise of Christ's presence as we live out the Great Commission. Our fears and challenges today probably differ greatly from those faced by John Paton, but the words of Christ are the same. Go. Make disciples. Baptize believers. Teach Christ's commands (Matthew 28:19–20).

We, like Paton, should take godly risks. If the words of Christ do not stir us to do what is naturally uncomfortable for us, we are taking neither His commands nor His promises seriously. God does not call His people to a life of ease. He calls them to spiritual warfare. We are soldiers of Christ, not pampered, spiritual elites. Opposition, misunderstanding, and even danger will come to those who strive to live like Christ and make a difference for Him in an evil world.

Throughout the fight, even when we seem to stand alone, we are never alone. Christ is with us always—through all time and in every place. Nothing can separate us from the love of Christ or the presence of Christ. Though hell should rage against us, Christ will build His church, never forsaking His people as His banner ever surges forward through the flames.

We are immortal until the work God has given us is done. Nothing can touch us until the time appointed by God. When that time comes, nothing can keep us from joining our Savior. John Paton's peaceful death in Victoria, Australia, at age eighty-two attests to this truth.

PERSONAL REFLECTION

- If I truly believed that I am immortal until my work is done, how would this conviction change the way I make decisions?

- What verses bring me hope when I need assurance of the presence of God?

- When has the presence of God been the dearest to me?

FURTHER READING   **Daniel 3**

Paton, John Gibson. *The Story of John G. Paton: Thirty Years Among South Sea Cannibals.* New York: A. L. Burt Company, 1892.

DAY 5

WE NEED
NOT FEAR

"We need not fear the result of trusting Him."

—JOHN STAM, MISSIONARY TO CHINA (1907–1934)

*"According to my earnest expectation and my hope, that in
nothing I shall be ashamed, but that with all boldness, as
always, so now also Christ shall be magnified in my body,
whether it be by life, or by death. For to me to live is Christ,
and to die is gain."*

—PHILIPPIANS 1:20–21

W here are you going?' asked the postmaster, when he recognized the prisoners.

'We don't know where they are going,' John answered simply, 'but we are going to heaven.'"[1]

As he spoke those words, John Stam knew the likelihood of survival was small. A chaotic war had sprung up in the Anhui province of China in 1934. Rough soldiers seized John and his wife Betty. They were missionaries on their first term, only in their late twenties. Writing to his mission, John explained their predicament and ended his brief letter roughly quoting Philippians 1:20: "The Lord bless and guide you, and as for us, may God be glorified whether by life or by death."[2] Days later, on a lonely hill outside the village, their captors beheaded the young couple.

The promises of God's Word had long prepared John and Betty Stam for this day. During his graduation speech at the Moody Bible Institute just two and a half years before, John spoke of the risks before them:

> Shall we retreat and turn back from our high calling in Christ Jesus; or dare we advance at God's command in face of the impossible? . . . Let us remind ourselves that the Great Commission was never qualified by clauses calling for advance only if funds were plentiful and no hardship or self-denial involved. On the contrary, we are told to expect tribulation and even persecution, but with it victory in Christ. . . . The faithfulness of God is the only certain thing in the world today. We need not fear the result of trusting Him.[3]

His wife, Betty, expressed the same faith in God's promises. At a Bible conference in 1925, Betty chose Philippians 1:21 as her life verse.[4] A few years later while studying at Moody Bible Institute, she prayed,

> Lord, I give up my own plans and purposes, all my own desires, hopes and ambitions, and I accept Thy will for my life. I give up myself, my life, my all, utterly to Thee, to be Thine forever. I hand over to Thy keeping all of my friendships; all the people whom I love are to take second place in my heart. Fill me now and seal me with Thy Spirit. Work out Thy whole will in my life at any cost, *for to me to live is Christ.* Amen.[5]

Both John and Betty viewed their deaths as gain and victory. That testimony stands engraved on their tombstone not far from where the soldiers' swords ended their lives. A single gravestone marks both graves. A cross at the center separates their epitaphs. To the left reads "John Cornelius Stam, 18 Jan. 1907; 'That Christ may be magnified by life or by death,' Phil. 1:20." To the right reads: "Elisabeth Scott Stam, his wife, 22 Feb. 1906; 'For me to live is Christ and to die is gain,' Phil. 1:21." Inscribed beneath the cross is the date and place of their martyrdom: "8 December 1934, Miaosheo, Anhui."

The spirit of Philippians 1:20–21 resounds from a poem treasured by Betty Stam, recorded in Mrs. Howard Taylor's account of their martyrdom, and circulated after their deaths. Just three years earlier, missionary E. H. Hamilton penned these words as he pondered the martyrdom of his colleague, Jack Vinson:

Afraid? Of what?
To feel the spirit's glad release?
To pass from pain to perfect peace,
The strife and strain of life to cease?
Afraid? Of that?

Afraid? Of what?
Afraid to see the Saviour's face,
To hear His welcome, and to trace,
The glory gleam from wounds of grace,
Afraid? Of that?

Afraid? Of what?
A flash—a crash—a pierced heart;
Brief darkness—Light—O Heaven's art!
A wound of His a counterpart!
Afraid? Of that?

Afraid? Of what?
To enter into Heaven's rest,
And yet to serve the Master blessed?
From service good to service best?
Afraid? Of that?

Afraid? Of what?
To do by death what life could not—
Baptize with blood a stony plot,
Till souls shall blossom from the spot?
Afraid? Of that?[6]

Both John's and Betty's families, though grieving for their losses, expressed faith in God's wisdom in allowing the martyrdom of their children. They found comfort in the promises of God. Their written responses just after hearing the news reflected their confidence that "to be absent from the body" is "to be present with the Lord" (2 Corinthians 5:8).

In a telegram to the China Inland Mission, Betty's father wrote, "Deeply appreciate your consolation. Sacrifice seems great, but not too great for Him who gave Himself for us. Experiencing God's grace. Believe wholeheartedly Romans 8:28."[7]

John's father echoed this same faith in God's promises, saying,

What could be more glorious? It is true, the manner in which they were sent out of this world was a shock to us all, but whatever of suffering they may have endured is now past, and they are both infinitely blessed with the joys of heaven. . . . We are sure that our dear brother and sister, Dr. and Mrs. C. E. Scott, both join us in saying, "The Lord gave, and the Lord hath taken away; blessed be the name of the Lord."[8]

The promises of God not only strengthened the faith of those martyred but also comforted the loved ones they left behind.

Truly, "we need not fear the result of trusting Him."

PERSONAL REFLECTION

- What is my biggest fear if I follow God? What promises of God can help me to overcome that fear and obey God anyway?

- If the worst-case scenario occurred for me or my family, what would that reveal about my faith in God?

- How does God's promise that to "be with Christ" is "far better" shape my view of death? Do I believe this is true even in the case of an "early" death?

- Am I willing for God to decide what is best for my life?

FURTHER READING   **Philippians 1**

Taylor, Mrs. Howard. *The Triumph of John and Betty Stam.* Philadelphia: China Inland Mission, 1935.

GIVE ME A WORK

*"I requested of my Lord and Master to give me a work,
I did not care how mean it was, only to try and
see how good I would do it."*

—GEORGE LIELE, MISSIONARY TO JAMAICA (c. 1750–1820)

*"Now unto him that is able to do exceeding abundantly above all
that we ask or think, according to the power that worketh in us."*

—EPHESIANS 3:20

The sharp clip-clop of horse hooves resounded through the meeting place. The crowd of worshipers, kidnapped from Africa to serve on plantations in Jamaica, nervously parted to let the colonial planter through. Pastor George Liele looked up from the bread and cup of the Lord's Table as the intruder bullied his way forward.

"Come, old Liele, give my horse the sacrament!" A string of curses followed.

"No sir, you are not fit yourself to receive it."

No one moved.

After a few tense moments, the colonial planter turned his horse and left the way he had come.[1]

In eighteenth-century society, Liele expected such confrontations. Born a slave around 1750 in Virginia, Liele grew up in servitude. In 1770 his master, Henry Sharpe, a British loyalist, moved him and his family to Georgia. Three years later, while attending Buckhead Creek Baptist Church with his master's family, Liele heard the gospel and trusted Christ as his Savior. He was soon baptized and accepted into the membership of this church made up of both colonials and slaves.

At that time, Liele also offered his life to the service of Christ. He later wrote, "I full well recollect, I requested of my Lord and Master to give me a work, I did not care how mean it was, only to try and see how good I would do it."[2] God would work abundantly beyond Liele's wildest expectations.

Liele immediately began preaching among his fellow slaves. His church, recognizing God's blessing on his ministry, licensed Liele to preach. Soon after, his master freed him from slavery to pursue the Lord's work.

In 1775, just two years into his itinerant ministry, Liele helped to establish the Silver Bluff Church. This church, located just across the South Carolina border from Augusta, Georgia, was probably the first African-American church in America. Liele continued preaching in plantations until the War for Independence forced him to settle down. In 1778, he and his family moved into British-occupied Savannah where he organized and pastored the First African Baptist Church.

With the British defeat in 1783 and the uncertainty of the war's aftermath, Liele decided to emigrate to Jamaica. He indentured himself to a family of British loyalists to pay his family's travel expenses.[3] Together, they sailed to Kingston, Jamaica. Though a free man himself, Liele built his home near the colonial plantations where slaves from Africa labored. To support his family, he worked as a farmer and transported goods by horse and wagon.[4]

As he had in Georgia, Liele preached the gospel. Soon, he had planted a church near Kingston. As the work grew to the surrounding plantations, Liele recruited men to become preachers and pastors.

Liele's training ministry followed a pattern begun years before in the American colonies with a man named David George. Liele led George to Christ and mentored him. Not long after, David George became the pastor of the newly formed Silver Bluff Church. Around the time Liele left the United States for Jamaica, David George emigrated to Nova Scotia for about ten years before finally settling in Sierra Leone, planting churches wherever he went.[5]

In Jamaica, Liele sought disciples in the mold of David George to multiply the work. Under Liele's ministry, the Lord recruited His own servants from among the slaves and former slaves of Jamaica, including George Gibbs and Moses Baker. Soon, new assemblies of believers spread across the island.[6]

By 1791, Liele wrote to a friend in England of 500 professions of faith. By 1814 and the belated arrival of the first British missionary to Jamaica, 8,000 slaves had already trusted Christ as their Savior, and many churches dotted the plantations. In the face of discrimination, disrespect, and violence, the work would continue to grow even after Liele's death. By 1832, 20,000 in Jamaica would claim the name of Christ.[7]

God answered Liele's prayer: He gave him a work and blessed it beyond what he could ever have dreamed. Ten years before William Carey left Britain for India and twenty-nine years before Adoniram Judson left New England for Burma, Liele left Georgia to reach Jamaica with the gospel. Among a despised and abused people, he faithfully served the Lord in poor physical conditions but with amazing spiritual results.

Liele left behind a shining example for those yearning to be used of God. First, he was willing to do "mean things" for God. In the late eighteenth century, the word *mean* described low social or economic status. Liele was content to remain poor, working among slaves, to do the Lord's work. Second, Liele committed to "try and see how good I would do it." This is the attitude of Colossians 3:23: "And whatsoever ye do, do it heartily, as to the Lord, and not unto men." This mindset is rooted in the goal of 1 Corinthians 10:31: "Whether therefore ye eat, or drink, or whatsoever ye do, do all to the glory of God." God honored Liele's humble devotion by blessing him with a bountiful harvest.

Today, God continues to defy the odds as He transforms and empowers those whom the world ignores. He's seeking humble believers who are willing to serve wherever He leads. As God promises in Ephesians 3:20–21, He can do "exceeding abundantly above all that we ask or think, according to the power that worketh in us." Surrender yourself for His use. Plead with God: "Give me a work! Use me in such a way that You alone get the glory for all that is done. Amen."

PERSONAL REFLECTION

- Do I long for God to use me?
- If I prayed, "Lord, give me a work," am I afraid of what God might give me? Why?
- What would keep me from embracing a lower standard of living in order to reach others for Christ?
- If others consider the work God gives me to be insignificant, what promises of God's Word can I claim to help me stay faithful?

FURTHER READING   Isaiah 6

DAY 7

---◀---

DONE ON
OUR KNEES

"Solid, lasting missionary work is done on our knees."

—JAMES O. FRASER, MISSIONARY TO CHINA (1886–1938)

"The effectual fervent prayer of a righteous man availeth much."

—JAMES 5:16

Mist rolled over the jagged peaks near the border between China and Burma. Tiptoeing along cliffside paths and scaling the heights like a mountain goat, twenty-four-year-old James O. Fraser struggled to reach the remote villages of the Lisu people. In 1910, no modern roads penetrated the gorges of southwest Yunnan. Few besides the Lisu themselves climbed these treacherous mountains.

Though often welcomed by the Lisu people, Fraser felt opposition to his message. Years of tradition, demonic oppression, and opium addiction bound the people. Fraser brought the first rays of God's light into the region.

Though a man of prayer himself, Fraser felt the need for the intercession of other believers on behalf of the work. The initial response among the Lisu was slow. Increasingly, Fraser felt his weakness and need for Christ's grace.

In January 1913, Fraser wrote to his mother:

> I know you will never fail me in the matter of intercession, but will you think and pray about getting a group of like-minded friends, whether few or many, whether in one place or scattered, to join in the same petitions? If you could form a small prayer circle I would write regularly to the members.[1]

A handful of his mother's friends in England launched Fraser's first prayer circle. Over time, the prayer circle grew. To encourage them, Fraser wrote, "Solid, lasting missionary work is done on our knees. What I covet more than anything is earnest, believing prayer, and I write to ask you to continue to put up much prayer for me and the work here."[2]

As his prayer circle interceded for him, Fraser continued working and waiting for fruit among the Lisu. "Preparation, delay, and growth are the characteristics of God's working both in history and in nature," he wrote in 1918. "We cannot fret souls into the Kingdom of Heaven; neither, when they are once converted, can we worry them into maturity."[3] Remembering these principles, Fraser quoted Lamentations 3:26: "It is good that a man should both hope and quietly wait for the salvation of the LORD."

By 1919, Fraser had begun to experience the positive effect of increased prayer on the fruitfulness of the work. Therefore, he determined to pursue more prayer partners. He wrote,

> Knowing as I do the conditions of the work, its magnitude (potentially), its difficulties and the opposition it meets with, I have definitely resolved, with God's help, to enlarge the place of my tent; to lengthen

my prayer cords and strengthen my intercessory stakes [notice Fraser's repeated allusions to Isaiah 54:2]. I have, that is to say, resolved to make a forward movement with regard to the Prayer Circle.[4]

Rather than mail one letter to be shared among the group of ten in the prayer circle, he began sending each member their own copy. At the time, this was a significant additional expenditure, but given the power of prayer, a worthy one. Fraser challenged his faithful prayer warriors to circulate his letters among their godly friends, forming their own prayer circles for the work in China.

Fraser firmly believed the results he had begun to see were directly related to the increase in prayer. In a letter to his prayer circles in 1919, Fraser wrote,

> I cannot insist too strongly on my own helplessness among these people apart from the grace of God. Although I have been now ten years in China and have had considerable experience with both Chinese and Lisu, I find myself able to do little or nothing apart from God's going before me and working among them. Without this I feel like a man who has his boat grounded in shallow water. Pull or push as he may, he will not be able to make his boat move more than a few inches. But let the tide come in and lift his boat off the bottom—then he will be able to move it as far as he pleases, quite easily and without friction.[5]

Empowered by intercessory prayer, Fraser traveled constantly and taught in smoky shacks throughout the peaks and valleys of the Salween. His abilities in the local dialect increased to the point that he took on the task of reducing the language into writing. His work came to be known as the "Fraser script." Eventually, a few families trusted Christ. Then, by 1920, entire villages made professions of faith.

Fraser's writings frequently emphasize the necessity of prayer in the arduous process of bearing spiritual fruit:

The longer the preparation [of God working in hearts through intercessory prayer], the deeper the work. The deeper the root, the firmer the plant when once it springs above ground. I do not believe that any deep work of God takes root without long preparation somewhere.[6]

To his prayer circles, he wrote, "If I am sure of anything, it is that your prayers have made a very real difference to my life and service."[7] In 1922, he wrote, "I used to think that prayer should have the first place and teaching the second. I now feel it would be truer to give prayer the first, second, and third place, and teaching the fourth."[8]

In 1923 and 1924, Fraser furloughed in Britain and North America. During this time, he championed the cause of prayer among his supporters and his mission. At his urging, the China Inland Mission launched the Prayer Companionship of the Mission. Following Fraser's example, this initiative encouraged missionaries and their supporters to form prayer circles of ten people to partner together in detailed, faith-filled prayer for individual missionaries. Soon, over 3,000 prayer warriors joined the cause.[9]

During his furlough, at a conference in the state of Washington, Fraser met a young believer named Isobel Miller. After the conference, her father invited Fraser to stay with the family in Vancouver. Fraser's testimony, fueled by his prayer life, made a deep impression on Isobel.[10] She would later marry John Kuhn, and together they would continue the work Fraser had begun with the Lisu.

In 2018, this author had dinner with a group of Lisu pastors and church workers. The men spoke only Mandarin and their local dialect. I did not know Fraser's name in Chinese, but I asked them whether they had ever heard of Fraser. Immediately, the men smiled and tried to all answer at once. Fraser's name was one of the few English words they knew.

"Yes! He led my grandparents to Christ!"

"We all know of him. Whole villages of Lisu today claim to be Christian because of his work."

Fraser's prayers and the prayers of his multiplying prayer circles reflect the truth of God's promise in James 5:16: "The effectual fervent prayer of a righteous man availeth much." Any fruit from his labors Fraser attributed to God's work through prayer. What a lasting work the Lord built on the prayers of His people!

PERSONAL REFLECTION

- How much time do I spend in prayer daily? Does the time I spend in prayer each day reflect how dependent I am on God?

- If I am content to serve God without relying on prayer, what does this tell me about my spiritual life?

- Would I even notice if I stopped praying? Would anyone else?

- What percentage of my prayers are intercession for others? Do these prayers include intercession for the gospel's advance through fellow believers and missionaries?

- Am I humble enough to ask others to pray for me?

FURTHER READING   **Ephesians 6:10–20**

Taylor, Mrs. Howard. *Behind the Ranges: Fraser of Lisuland.* London: Lutterworth Press and the China Inland Mission, 1944.

DAY 8

PLAIN, UNVARNISHED HARD WORK

"Life does contain moments of adventure, but these times are interspersed with long periods of plain, unvarnished hard work. The real things in life are attained at these monotonous level periods, so to speak, more than they are at the high peaks of excitement." [1]

—ISOBEL KUHN, MISSIONARY TO CHINA (1901–1957)

"Labour not for the meat which perisheth, but for that meat which endureth unto everlasting life."

—JOHN 6:27

A noble life is not a blaze of sudden glory won. But just an adding up of days in which good work is done." [2]

"Rubbish," thought young Canadian Isobel Miller. The blaze of glory attracted her. Reveling in the party life of the 1920s, Isobel found no value in the short poem her grandmother had copied for her from the newspaper. [3] She determined to live life to the fullest. However, God would save her soul and show her the path to an abundant life of which she had never dreamed—a life of faithful work for the cause of Christ.

As Isobel grew in her faith, God used Mrs. Howard Taylor's two-volume biography of Hudson Taylor to draw her into missions. These books, filled with accounts of trials and faith, inspired her to dream of joining the China Inland Mission. In her exuberance, maybe she did not see the labors ahead.

However, James O. Fraser, veteran missionary with the China Inland Mission, warned Isobel of the arduous work of a missionary. Isobel first met Fraser in 1923 at a missions conference called The Firs in Bellingham, Washington. Afterward, her parents invited Fraser to stay with them in Vancouver for a few days. Along a rocky Canadian seashore, Fraser spoke frankly of the loneliness and suffering that often accompany serving God. Isobel later wrote,

> I believe now that he did it deliberately to sift me. If I were truly called of God, I would not be discouraged by plain talk about the cost. If I were not called by God, but just had romantic notions of a foreign land, the sooner my gossamer dream wafted away the better.[4]

Isobel was undeterred.

The next September, Isobel resigned from her teaching position and enrolled in the Moody Bible Institute. By 1928, she boarded a ship for China where she joined her former Moody classmate and fiancé, John Kuhn. The next year, she and John married in Kunming, Yunnan. Her work had only just begun.

Despite Fraser's warnings, the sheer work and cultural differences shocked Isobel. She would write, "I went to China eager and hopeful to be a soul winner. I was ridiculously, pathetically unprepared for the cost."[5] She found, like many missionaries past and present, that everyday life in a foreign culture sucks away time for ministry. The battle for hygiene where cleanliness is not valued, the time stolen by travel where transportation is inconvenient, and the equilibrium-altering intrusions of the unexpected shatter the idealistic fervor of youthful dreams. What was once novel and adventurous becomes odious drudgery.

To make matters worse, Isobel found her evangelistic efforts to be nearly fruitless. Stubborn determination led to exhaustion but little spiritual headway. She wrote,

> I had worked faithfully. There was not a hamlet or a village on that whole plain where I had not personally gone, driven off their various dogs, pushed my way into their dirty courtyards and presented my message. The women were kind and everyone was nice to me but only a mere handful of people had accepted Christ. And most of these were very poor illiterate women—too weak to call a church.[6]

She wrote of her prayers during her early time with the Chinese: "I expressed my willingness to be put on the shelf, willing not to be the one He used, if only I might see Him work!"[7]

Even later, as Isobel found her niche in missions work among the Lisu and saw God work in their ministry, the hard work did not abate. Long gone were the comforts of suburban Vancouver. Days of trekking through rustic mountains or jostling in trucks on rough roads marked her life. Bean curd, pork fat, and animal products not thought to be food in the West filled her diet. Daily survival robbed time for ministry, but the young woman plodded on.

Isobel had her eyes on the prize. She labored for the eternal. She took the words of Christ seriously when He said, "Labour not for the meat which perisheth, but for that meat which endureth unto everlasting life" (John 6:27). Eternal results come, not through a flash of brilliance, but by persistent labor in the power of Christ.

Isobel came to realize that "life does contain moments of adventure, but these times are interspersed with long periods of plain, unvarnished hard work. The real things in life are attained at these monotonous level periods, so to speak, more than they are at the high peaks of excitement."[8]

Life means work. Lasting results usually require years of plodding. However, the time and energy spent are neither wasted nor worthless. Faithfulness in both the mundane and the spiritual lead to eternal rewards.

PERSONAL REFLECTION

- For whom do I work? For self? For future leisure? For family? For God?

- How can I find value in the mundane chores of daily living like homework, cleaning, cooking, laundry, and home repair?

- What blessings am I missing because I wish God had placed some other work before me today?

- How could these laborious obstacles be turned to opportunities?

FURTHER READING   **2 Thessalonians 3**

Kuhn, Isobel. *By Searching: My Journey Through Doubt Into Faith.* Chicago: Moody Press, 1959.

DAY 9

I AM NOTHING

*"I see I am nothing, and can do nothing
without help from above."*

**—DAVID BRAINERD, MISSIONARY TO NATIVE AMERICANS
(1718–1747)**

*"But to this man will I look, even to him that is poor and of
a contrite spirit, and trembleth at my word."*

—ISAIAH 66:2

He has no more grace than this chair!" said twenty-three-year-old David Brainerd. He quickly regretted these words. The administration of Yale University promptly expelled the student, who in the fervor following George Whitefield's revivals, accused his professor of lacking genuine regeneration. Brainerd's expulsion from Yale blocked his path toward a respectable New England pastorate.

To some observers, Brainerd's résumé reads like one failure after another. Expelled from university. Called to preach to a people many of his contemporaries despised. Spent four years on horseback wandering the wilderness of New York, Pennsylvania, and New Jersey. Battled chronic tuberculosis. Continued preaching anyway to a largely antagonistic audience. Endured ever-worsening attacks of his disease. Suffered depression and cataloged it mercilessly in his journal. Kept traveling, kept preaching, and kept journaling until he died of tuberculosis at age twenty-nine. With such a life story, why do we remember and respect David Brainerd today?

After Brainerd passed away in the home of Jonathan Edwards, the famous preacher and theologian compiled *The Life of David Brainerd*. Arguably the first missionary biography ever published, this book would never go out of print. The testimony of Brainerd's short life would inspire and encourage countless others to give their lives for the cause of Christ. The list of those who specifically pointed to the influence of this biography of Brainerd includes such key figures as John Wesley, William Carey, Henry Martyn, Robert Morrison, David Livingstone, Robert Murray M'Cheyne, Andrew Murray, and Jim and Elisabeth Elliot.

Edwards, in his preface to the biography, holds Brainerd up as an example for all believers, but he cautions that only Christ is a perfect example:

> The example of Jesus Christ is the only example that ever existed in human nature as altogether perfect; which therefore is a rule to try all other examples by; and the dispositions, frames, and practices of others must be commended and followed no further, than they were followers of Christ.[1]

To further make this point, Edwards then lists some of Brainerd's most obvious faults: the young man struggled with periods of depression and overworked himself to the detriment of his health. Toward the end of his life, Brainerd admonished his brother to take care of his health, admitting that he had not done so himself.

However, through these faults, a spiritual depth and a fervent passion for God shone through. Brainerd's journals ring with emotional outbursts of dedication to God. In one entry, he attests, "I hardly ever so longed to live to God, and to be altogether devoted to him; I wanted to wear out my life in his service, and for his glory."[2] Later, he wrote, "Was again melted with desires that God might be glorified, and with longings to love and live to him."[3]

His heart's cries have resonated with like-minded saints throughout the past three centuries. Brainerd's genuine struggles made him real and accessible. He was no hero on some higher plane than the ordinary believer. In his biography, some form of the word *weakness* occurs 150 times, mostly in direct quotations from his journals. He repeats the word *nothing* 120 times, often referring to himself. For example, he writes, "I never felt it so sweet to be nothing, and less than nothing, and to be accounted nothing."[4] Brainerd employs the word *glory* or *glorify* 142 times, highlighting his passion for glorifying God. Young men and women since his day have seen his genuine brokenness, authentic humility, and burning passion for the glory of God, awakening in them a spiritual hunger and holy ambition to be used of God.

Judging from the spirit of his journals, Brainerd did not crave such influence. He wrote, "I felt a great desire, that all God's people might know how mean and little and vile I am; that they might see I am nothing . . . so they might pray for me aright, and not have the least dependence upon me."[5] However, God delights to use the weak, and He chose to use Brainerd as a realistic example of what He can do despite the physical, emotional, and even spiritual frailties of His people. This exhibition of God's strength in human weakness—even more so than the dozens of Native Americans he led to the Lord—is Brainerd's legacy. While Brainerd probably would have been horrified by his posthumous celebrity status, he would have been gratified to see how God has been glorified through his life and death.

If God could use Brainerd despite his youthful indiscretion, despite what many today would consider an emotional disorder, despite his lack of career opportunities, and despite his frequent illnesses, can He not use me? What overcame these deficiencies and disadvantages was Brainerd's passion for and dependence on God.

Brainerd was a living example of the man God promises to consider. In Isaiah 66:2, God says, "To this man will I look, even to him that is poor and of a contrite spirit." Brainerd's journals give us a glimpse into his private, devotional life where we find the kind of heart God can mold and use for His glory.

PERSONAL REFLECTION

- If someone caught a glimpse of my walk with God, would they be inspired to emulate my example? Why?

- How does my desire for God's glory shine through my efforts to serve Him?

- Am I willing to admit that I am nothing without Christ?

FURTHER READING   **2 Corinthians 4**

Edwards, Jonathan. *The Life and Diary of David Brainerd with Notes and Reflections.* Peabody, MA: Hendrickson, 2006.

Christie, Vance. *David Brainerd: A Flame for God.* Greanies House, UK: Christian Focus, 2009.

BE ALL THERE

"Wherever you are, be all there. Live to the hilt every situation you believe to be the will of God."

—JIM ELLIOT, MISSIONARY TO ECUADOR (1927–1956)

"Therefore, my beloved brethren, be ye stedfast, unmoveable, always abounding in the work of the Lord, forasmuch as ye know that your labour is not in vain in the Lord."

—1 CORINTHIANS 15:58

I dare not stay home," wrote Jim Elliot as he mulled the decision to leave the U.S. for the Quichua region of Ecuador. The challenge of taking the gospel to the Waorani, a Stone Age people group untouched by Western civilization, thrilled him.[1] From that moment until the day the spears of the Waorani ended his life, Elliot focused on the task. Yet, Elliot had learned the importance of commitment long before leaving for the jungle of South America.

For two years after his 1949 graduation from Wheaton College, Elliot endured a prolonged waiting period. Elliot knew that God wanted him to serve overseas, but he waited on the Lord for where that would be: India or South America? Elliot knew whom he would marry, if he married: Elisabeth Howard. But he waited on God's timing, knowing that the primitive work he desired to pursue would probably demand a single man.

While he waited, Elliot worked in ministries and jobs he knew to be temporary. He followed the Lord's guidance to Oregon, Oklahoma, and then across the Midwest. At times, he taught school, ran evangelistic rallies, preached on the radio, and even worked in sales.[2] During this period of uncertainty, the Lord impressed on him the importance of commitment. In his journal, he exhorted himself, "Wherever you are, be all there! Live to the hilt every situation you believe to be the will of God."[3]

God demands our commitment. He calls for our wholehearted devotion. From the first books of the Bible to the last, God commands His people, "Thou shalt love the Lord thy God with all thy heart, and with all thy soul, and with all thy mind. This is the first and great commandment" (Matthew 22:37–38). In the Old Testament, Solomon exhorts, "Whatsoever thy hand findeth to do, do it with thy might; for there is no work, nor device, nor knowledge, nor wisdom, in the grave, whither thou goest" (Ecclesiastes 9:10).

No man knows how long he has. Jim Elliot did not know it, but he had only twenty-eight years on this earth. He wrote in his journal, "God, I pray, light these idle sticks of my life and may I burn up for Thee. Consume my life, my God, for it is Thine. I seek not a long life but a full one like Yours, Lord Jesus."[4] God gave him a full life. Jim was "all there."

In the New Testament, Paul repeats God's call to dedication: "And whatsoever ye do, do it heartily, as to the Lord, and not unto men" (Colossians 3:23). Every man will one day stand before God; so, wherever you are, be all there. Be all in. Be committed. Make a difference. Do not be a spectator; be a mover.

Elliot, as a college student in 1948, prayed, "Father, make me a 'crisis man.' Bring those I contact to decision. Let me not be a milepost on a single road. Make me a fork, so that men must turn one way or another on facing Christ in me."[5]

During his waiting period after university, Elliot read the diary of David Brainerd. The commitment and sacrifice of this missionary who died so early in his ministry, deeply impressed young Elliot. That same week, immersed in the testimony of Brainerd, Elliot famously wrote, "He is no fool who gives what he cannot keep to gain that which he cannot lose."[6] His words echo those of his Lord in Mark 8:35, "For whosoever will save his life shall lose it; but whosoever shall lose his life for my sake and the gospel's, the same shall save it." Elliot died how he lived: He was all there. The passion with which Elliot lived is the same passion with which he died, and neither his life, nor his death was in vain.

Maybe you feel that living such a passionate, "all there" life is extreme, maybe even reckless. After all, Elliot died on a remote beach in the jungles of Ecuador. However, God calls us to this kind of dedicated service. First Corinthians 15:58 exhorts us, "Therefore, my beloved brethren, be ye stedfast, unmoveable, always abounding in the work of the Lord, forasmuch as ye know that your labour is not in vain in the Lord."

What is the basis for such dedication? The promise of immortality in the preceding verses:

Behold, I shew you a mystery; We shall not all sleep, but we shall all be changed, In a moment, in the twinkling of an eye, at the last trump: for the trumpet shall sound, and the dead shall be raised incorruptible, and we shall be changed. For this corruptible must put on incorruption, and this mortal must put on immortality. So when this corruptible shall have put on incorruption, and this mortal shall have put on immortality, then shall be brought to pass the saying that is written, Death is swallowed up in victory. O death, where is thy sting? O grave, where is thy victory? The sting of death is sin; and the strength of sin is the law. But thanks be to God, which giveth us the victory through our Lord Jesus Christ. (1 Corinthians 15:51–57)

Based on this promise, we can live our lives with the dedication and passion God commands. We can be "all there." God has given us the victory. Death is a beginning, not an ending. Martyrdom is a triumph, not a tragedy. Sacrifice is gain, not loss. Labor for Christ is treasure, not vanity.

PERSONAL REFLECTION

- Am I wishing I was somewhere else or with someone else? Where? With whom? Why?

- Where am I today? Am I "all there"? If I were, what would that look like?

- Do I long for the future to the point that I live distracted in the present?

FURTHER READING   **1 Corinthians 15:51–58**

Elliot, Elisabeth. *The Shadow of the Almighty: The Life and Testament of Jim Elliot*. San Francisco: Harper Collins, 1958.

DAY 11

FAITHFUL
IN LITTLE

*"Sinners perishing all around me, and I almost panting to tell
the far heathen of Christ! Surely this is wrong."*

**—SARAH HALL BOARDMAN JUDSON, MISSIONARY TO BURMA
(1803–1845)**

"He that is faithful in that which is least is faithful also in much."

—LUKE 16:10

Sarah Hall never intended her poem to lead to her marriage. In the history of romantic poetry, her work could rank as the least romantic of all time. The following stanza is an excerpt from her poem that circulated through New England churches in 1823:

> To bear to the nations all wrapp'd in thick gloom,
> The lamp of the gospel—the message of love.
> But Wheelock now slumbers beneath the cold wave,
> And Colman lies low in the dark cheerless grave.[1]

James Colman, pioneer missionary to Burma and early coworker of Adoniram Judson, had died on the mission field in 1822. Just three years before, his fellow missionary, Edward Wheelock, had also passed away. As news spread of yet another young missionary passing into glory, Christians throughout New England mourned. In Salem, Massachusetts, Sarah Hall, a teenager burdened for the cause of foreign missions, added her poetic eulogy.

George Boardman had never met Sarah Hall. He had heard of Colman's passing, and God moved him to take the fallen missionary's place in Burma. He left a promising position in the academic world and joined Adoniram Judson's organization, the Board of Foreign Missions. As he made preparations, he wondered what woman would possibly agree to marry him, given the untimely deaths of his predecessors in Burma. Sensing a kindred spirit in the author of the Colman poem, Boardman sought out Sarah Hall. On July 4, 1825, George Boardman and Sarah Hall married.

Just five years before, Sarah had trusted Christ as her Savior.[2] As she grew in the Lord, she read the biography of recently-deceased missionary Samuel Mills.[3] Mills' passion for reaching the downtrodden—the poor of New York, the Native Americans of the south, and the African slaves across America—inspired her. Sarah's writings of this period begin to show an intense yearning to take the gospel to those who had never heard:

> It is my ardent desire . . . that the glorious work of reformation may extend till every knee shall bow to the living God. For this expected, this promised era, let us pray earnestly, unceasingly, and with faith. How can I be so inactive, when I know that thousands are perishing in this land of grace; and millions in other lands are at this very moment kneeling before senseless idols![4]

However, her tender conscience convicted her of dreaming of leading people to Christ overseas while ignoring those closest to her. In her journal, she wrote, "Sinners perishing all around me, and I almost panting to tell the far heathen of Christ! Surely this is wrong. I will no longer indulge the vain foolish wish, but endeavor to be useful in the position where Providence has placed me."[5]

Thus moved by God, Sarah began sharing the gospel with the poor children of her town, starting a Sunday school ministry. At home, she urged her twelve younger siblings to trust in Christ. Even later, when serving in Burma, she would write her siblings, pleading with them to believe. In correspondence to her brother, she asked, "My brother, have you a heart to pray to God? Have you repented and turned to him? Or are you all careless and indifferent respecting your precious soul?"[6]

Sarah Hall lived out the biblical principle that faithfulness in little leads to faithfulness in much (Luke 16:10). Do you want to be used of God to do great things? You must first be humble enough to be used of God to do seemingly small things. In so doing, you will find that the small things may not be as small as you originally thought and that the large things may not be as great as you at first supposed. Faithfulness leads to opportunity for greater faithfulness. Sarah's example brings this principle to life.

In 1825, mere weeks after her marriage to George Boardman, Sarah sailed away from New England forever. In Burma, through much sickness, loss, and hardship, God would entrust the new couple with a fruitful work among the Karen people. God had equipped George and Sarah to take the gospel to the Karen tribe and had prepared the Karens to receive it. With joy, the young missionaries saw sixty-eight people from this unreached tribe come to Christ, the firstfruits of a greater harvest in the following years.[7]

By mid-1830, Sarah knew that her husband, like Colman whom he had replaced, would have but a short ministry. His body, wracked by a persistent cough, was wasting away. Sarah wrote to her sister, "Oh what desolation and anguish of spirit do I feel, when I think it is possible that in a few more months, my earthly guide, supporter, and delight, may be no more!"[8] The night before his death in February of 1831, Karen believers carried George to see the baptism of thirty-four new believers.[9] Boardman left this world, but the work he spearheaded among the Karens went on.

Due to the growing Karen ministry, Sarah chose to stay in Burma with her young son, George, rather than return to New England.[10] For the next three years, she continued teaching in a small school for girls in the town of Tavoy. Periodically, the young widow and her son braved the tiger-infested jungle to extend the gospel into remote Karen villages.[11]

Then in 1834, Sarah's ministry and influence expanded when she married widower Adoniram Judson, the leader of the work in Burma. In addition to the Karen work, she now ministered to Burmese and Peguan peoples. God used Sarah to translate John Bunyan's *Pilgrim's Progress* into Burmese and the New Testament into the Peguan language.

Great works for God begin with small acts of faithfulness. Sarah's faithfulness as a teenager laid the groundwork for greater opportunities for ministry in the future. From a local Sunday school for poor children to the evangelization of the unreached in Burma, her faithful service to God, wherever He placed her, glorified God.

What God did through Sarah Boardman Judson, He can do through believers today. Begin where you are now—this is your mission field. Be faithful in little things. Endure adversity by God's grace. Let God use you however and wherever He pleases.

PERSONAL REFLECTION

· What opportunities for serving God and others has God placed before me today? How faithful am I with these opportunities?

· Based on my current habits in my service to God, could I be entrusted with a greater work for God?

FURTHER READING   **Matthew 25:14–30**

DAY 12

---◀---

THEY WENT BACK

*"I seized them [the promises of God], acted on them,
and in acting discovered the Rock beneath."*

—ELISABETH ELLIOT, MISSIONARY TO ECUADOR (1926–2015)

*"He that dwelleth in the secret place of the most High shall
abide under the shadow of the Almighty. I will say of the* LORD*,
He is my refuge and my fortress: my God; in him will I trust."*

—PSALM 91:1–2

Why did they go back? How could they go back?

Darlene Deibler, a widow at age twenty-six, had every reason to stay in the U.S. She had sacrificed enough. She followed her husband, Russell Deibler, to the Wissel Lakes of Papua, Indonesia, only to be captured by the Japanese invaders during World War II. Her husband died in a Japanese prisoner-of-war camp. She herself only just survived, gaunt with malnutrition. Yet, three years later, she married Gerald Rose, and together they went back to Indonesia and served for nearly thirty years.

Sarah Boardman, a widow at age twenty-eight, had every reason to leave Burma. Two of her children and then her husband had passed away. Nearly every other woman in her era would have returned as a hero to her homeland. Instead, she and her young son George stayed among the Karen people in Burma. Sarah wrote to her family not long after her husband's death:

> Perhaps you think such intelligence [of revival in America] makes me wish to return. But no, my dear brothers and sisters, it makes me feel just the reverse. I do most ardently long to labor in this dark land till the day dawns upon us . . . rather I should say till the Sun of Righteousness reaches the meridian of Burmah, for the day has already dawned, and the eastern Karen mountains, enveloped for ages past in midnight gloom, are rejoicing in his bright beams.[1]

For three years as a widow, Sarah Boardman braved tiger-infested jungles continuing the Karen work. After her marriage to Adoniram Judson, she remained serving faithfully in Burma for eleven more years until her death.

Elisabeth Elliot, a widow at age twenty-nine, had every reason to leave Ecuador forever. No reasonable person would condemn her for harboring bitterness toward the tribesmen who had murdered her husband and his coworkers. No one would question whether she and her young daughter should return to South America. Of course, the young widow should stay in the United States. But she went back.

How could these women go back to the places where they had lost so much? Both Sarah and Elisabeth attested that their husbands' sacrifices only intensified their own burdens to return to their target people group and continue the work they had begun together. Sarah wrote, "My beloved husband wore out his life in this glorious cause; and that remembrance makes me more than ever attached to the work and the people for whose salvation he labored till death."[2] Similarly, Elisabeth Elliot explained, "The fact that Jesus Christ died for all makes me interested in the salvation of all, but the fact that Jim loved and died for the Aucas [Waorani] intensifies my love for them."[3] She later wrote, "I knew that if life was to go on, it must go on meaningfully."[4] For these women, living meaningfully meant going back to the place and people of their sorrows.

How could they do this?

First, these women knew that death is not the end. Elisabeth shared the same faith that motivated the five men martyred by the Waorani. She wrote, "They took quite literally the words 'The world passeth away, and the lust thereof, but he that doeth the will of God abideth forever.'"[5] She asked, "Is the distinction between living for Christ and dying for Him so great? Is not the second the logical conclusion of the first?"[6]

Second, these women followed God's leading in obedience, just as their husbands had. "Obedience, if it is a good reason for dying, is just as good a reason for living," wrote Elliot. "I knew that there was no other answer for me. The 'whys' that screamed themselves at me day and night could not be silenced, but I could live with them if I simply went on and did the next thing."[7] Sarah Boardman too obeyed her Lord while grieving her loss, explaining, "We have sixty scholars in town, and about fifty among the Karens in the jungles. I feel desolate, lonely, and sometimes deeply distressed at my great and irreparable loss,—but I bless God I am not in despair."[8] These missionaries got no free pass from the normal cycles of grief. If anything, the public attention amplified their loss. However, they did not see their sorrow as an excuse for sin. They obeyed.

Finally, these women made God their refuge. The Word of God, especially the Psalms, gave them strength.[9] Quoting from Psalm 91:1, Elisabeth, entitled her biography of her husband, *The Shadow of the Almighty*. When she made her first contact with the remote tribe that not long before had murdered her husband, she wrote, "He was to me that night, as the Psalmist said, a 'strong tower.'"[10] Elisabeth listed promises from the Psalms, saying, "I seized them, acted on them, and in acting discovered the Rock beneath."[11]

When the Waorani murdered a man from the very village where she and her daughter stayed, Elisabeth quoted Psalm 91:7: "A thousand shall fall at thy side, and ten thousand at thy right hand; but it shall not come nigh thee." She wrote,

> I found peace in the knowledge that I was in the hands of God. Not in the confidence that I was not going to be killed. Not in any false sense of security that God would protect me, any more than he had protected my husband, the four missionaries, or Honario [the murdered villager] from the wooden lances. Simply in knowing that He held my destiny in His two hands, and that He did what was right.[12]

Sharing of her safe arrival in a Waorani village for the first time, Elliot wrote, "Once more we had seen the Word of God worth trusting. He cannot prove this to us unless we act upon it."[13] She acted on the promises of God. In doing so, she faced great danger, but she rested on the character of the One who made the promises.

Upon her initial arrival in Burma, Sarah Boardman wrote, "Oh may this renewed assurance of his kind care, teach me confidence in his promises, and fill me with ardent desires to be constantly employed in his service."[14] The death of her husband changed none of her resolve to rely on God's promises, nor to continue in His service.

Similarly, Darlene Deibler, after years in the Japanese internment camp and the untimely death of her husband, testified of God's sustaining power. She, too, borrowed the words of Psalm 91, praying, "I have been safer here, overshadowed by Your love than I would have been anywhere else on this earth, outside of Your will!"[15] With that confidence, Darlene returned to Indonesia.

They went back. Could I?

The promises these women acted on are the same promises I read every day. The God of these promises is the same God I serve. Psalm 91 is no obscure passage filled with secrets for the spiritually elite. These women took common promises and simply lived them in their unique circumstances.

Do I truly believe God's promises? If I do, I must act on them, and this will inevitably incur godly risks. Elliot wrote, "There is no need for faith where there is no consciousness of an element of risk."[16] Where there is risk, you truly find out who you are trusting. When the supports are all gone, you see what is underneath. Is the Rock that Elisabeth, Sarah, and Darlene found beneath you?

PERSONAL REFLECTION

- How do my decisions and actions show that I truly trust God's promises?

- Does risk or uncertainty prevent me from doing what God wants me to do?

- How am I building my faith in God's promises today so that, when trials come, I can face them with confidence in God and His Word?

FURTHER READING   Psalm 91

Elliot, Elisabeth. *The Savage, My Kinsman.* Ann Arbor, MI: Servant Books, 1981.

Elliot, Elisabeth. *Through Gates of Splendor.* Wheaton, IL: Tyndale House, 1981.

EXPECTING THE IMPOSSIBLE

"No, sir . . . I expect God will."

—ROBERT MORRISON, FIRST MISSIONARY TO CHINA (1782–1834)

"Not by might, nor by power, but by my spirit,
saith the LORD of hosts."

—ZECHARIAH 4:6

In the dim light of his counting house near the New York harbor, the merchant sneered across the counter at twenty-five-year-old Robert Morrison. This determined Englishman had just booked passage on the *Trident*. A four-month voyage beginning in April 1807 would take the young missionary to Guangzhou, China (then called Canton).

The American merchant knew what the young man would face—storms in the Atlantic, peril around the horn of Africa, the possibility of pirates passing through the Indian Ocean, and a rough welcome on the Chinese shore. The authorities of the Qing dynasty resolutely resisted the incursion of foreigners into their land. They made stringent exceptions to this policy only for the sake of limited trade with the outside world.

The merchant understood why Morrison now stood before him. He could not sail directly from England to China. The powerful British East India Company controlled all shipping to the East and, in exchange for their exclusive trading rights with China, refused any application for passage to the country. With such restrictions in place, how would a missionary—the first ever to China—fare? The merchant pitied and scorned the naïve youth.

Morrison's friend, who accompanied him as he reserved his place on the ship, recounts the exchange:

> When all business matters were arranged, [the merchant] turned about from his desk and with a sardonic grin, addressing Morrison, said, "And so, Mr. Morrison, you really expect that you will make an impression on the idolatry of the great Chinese Empire?" "No, Sir," said Morrison, with more than his usual sternness, "I expect God will."[1]

Robert Morrison understood the truth of Zechariah 4:6: "Not by might, nor by power, but by my spirit, saith the LORD of hosts." This passage was written to those who, like Morrison and many today, face daunting odds and seemingly unsurmountable obstacles in their service to Christ.

The returning Jewish exiles from the Babylonian captivity who first heard the promise of Zechariah 4:6 grappled with overwhelming challenges: adapting to a foreign homeland, rebuilding demolished stone homes, enduring dire threats from enemies much stronger than they, and facing the daily insecurity of living in a city without a wall during a violent era. Upon arrival in Jerusalem, Zerubbabel, the Jewish governor, had led the former exiles in laying the foundation for a new temple. However, as pressure mounted, the people had stopped obeying God. They halted work on the temple. Now, fifteen years later, the temple foundation was a daily reminder of their spiritual failure.

The odds were too high. The risk too great. The job impossible.

God sent the prophets Haggai and Zechariah. They encouraged Israel to obey and serve God despite the obstacles. The prophecies and promises they preached still embolden believers today.

Not by might. Your physical strength will not get God's work done. Your determination will not propel you over the obstacles or produce the fruit God desires.

Nor by power. Your abilities will not get God's work done. Abilities are good, and God can use them. We should always be learning and growing, becoming more skilled and more usable to God. However, ultimately, no matter how skilled and experienced we become, our abilities will come up short. Paul, a uniquely gifted man, testifies to this truth in 2 Corinthians 4:7, saying, "But we have this treasure in earthen vessels, that the excellency of the power may be of God, and not of us."

But by My Spirit. Who's Spirit? The Spirit of the Lord of Hosts, the all-powerful (Zechariah 4:6), all-seeing (4:10), and all-encompassing Lord of the whole earth (4:14). God's people were outnumbered and over-matched by enemies on every side in a city whose walls had been reduced to rubble. As they faced these overwhelming odds, God reminded His people sixty-seven times in the books of Haggai and Zechariah that He is the "Lord of Hosts." This name of God encourages us that with God we are never a minority. He is Lord of the armies over heaven and earth. What is impossible to us is never impossible to Him. He encourages us today just as He encouraged Israel in 520 B.C.: "Be strong, all ye people of the land, saith the Lord, and work: for I am with you, saith the Lord of hosts: According to the word that I covenanted with you when ye came out of Egypt, so my spirit remaineth among you: fear ye not!" (Haggai 2:4–5).

We must rely on God's Spirit to give us the ability to do God's work. So often what God has called us to do seems impossible. The people of Israel stared at the impossible every time they passed the abandoned temple foundation amid the rubble of Jerusalem. Not long after the prophets encouraged them to rely on God's Spirit, God did what only He could do. God empowered His people as He promised, and they finished the temple (Zechariah 4:9). Though many of the Jews were disappointed by this new temple's appearance compared with the glory of Solomon's temple, they had laid important groundwork for the coming of their Messiah, Jesus Christ, several centuries later.

When Morrison died in 1834, nearly twenty-seven years after arriving in China, he too may have been disappointed in his life's work. To remain in China, he had been forced to work for the British East India Company, the very company that kept missionaries out of China. The first missionary to China planted no churches. He led only a handful of individuals to faith in Christ. His efforts to learn Chinese, translate materials into Chinese, and spread the gospel necessitated a life of hardship and separation. Morrison alternated between Macau and Guangzhou, frequently leaving his family for six months at a time, traveling in times of war, and suffering sickness in a harsh climate. When he attempted to publish his works, a fire in Guangzhou destroyed his printing paper, and later, religious enemies in Macau destroyed some of his printing equipment. White ants often devoured the supplies that survived. For much of Morrison's life, setbacks seemed more numerous than advances.

Despite all this, God used Morrison to pave the way for thousands of missionaries after him who would plant churches throughout all of China and win millions to Christ. Through God's Spirit, Morrison produced the first Chinese/English dictionary which allowed missionaries after him to learn the difficult language. He published tracts, doctrinal pamphlets, and a hymnbook in Chinese. Even more influential was his translation of the Bible which became the foundation for the Chinese Union Version, the Bible most Chinese Christians use today. Through Morrison, God made an indelible impression on the idolatry of the great Chinese empire which is felt today.

PERSONAL REFLECTION

- What gives me confidence that spiritually dead people with no interest in the things of God can leave their self-centered lifestyles to follow Christ?
- Are my expectations based on my abilities or on God's Spirit?
- How can I rely on the Holy Spirit in a greater way today?
- In what ways do my expectations for serving God or influencing others need to change?

FURTHER READING   **Zechariah 4**

Broomhall, Marshall. *Robert Morrison: A Master-Builder.* London: Student Christian Movement, 1927.

DAY 14

———— ◢ ————

NOT LIMITED

*"My Lord is not limited. He knows my present situation,
and He can supply all I need."*

**—GEORGE MÜLLER, IMMIGRANT PASTOR IN ENGLAND
(1805–1898)**

*"But seek ye first the kingdom of God, and his righteousness;
and all these things shall be added unto you."*

—MATTHEW 6:33

Please, sir, I want some more," said the hungry Oliver Twist, a fictional orphan of the early nineteenth century.[1] Consigned to workhouses, poor and orphaned children labored long hours in filthy, industrial buildings. The same deplorable conditions that inspired author Charles Dickens to publish the novel *Oliver Twist* in 1837 moved George Müller to open an orphanage two years earlier.

Müller originally came to England as a German missionary to the Jews in 1829. Not long after his arrival, he widened his ministry to both Jews and Gentiles, taking a pastorate just outside of London. The next year, he got married. Despite the economic volatility of the time, Müller felt led of the Lord to stop taking a salary, trusting God alone to provide his needs.

After a move to Bristol, the needs of begging children around the city reminded Müller of his time in Halle, Germany. For two months, just before he moved to Britain, he had boarded in rooms reserved for needy theological students at the orphanage founded by the famous pietist August Francke.[2] Could Müller open a similar establishment to help the children of Bristol? With no salary himself, how could he undertake the care of these penniless orphans?

On November 20, 1835, Müller discovered the biography of August Francke while visiting in a fellow Christian's home. He wrote in his journal, "I have frequently, for a long time, thought of laboring in a similar way, on a much smaller scale; not to imitate Francke, but in reliance upon the Lord."[3]

In addition to the plight of the orphans themselves, Müller saw a second, more pressing need. Many British believers worked excessively long hours to the detriment of their families and their own spiritual lives. Fear of ending up in the workhouses kept these believers from reducing their work hours so that they could spend time with God each day and order their lives according to God's Word. Müller believed that an orphanage supported by God alone with no public appeals for funds would be a shining example to strengthen the faith of these struggling believers.[4]

Müller wrote in his diary:

> I certainly did from my heart desire to be used by God to benefit the bodies of poor children bereaved of both parents, and seek, in other respects, with the help of God, to do them good for this life; I also particularly longed to be used by God in getting the dear orphans trained up in the fear of God; but still, the first and primary object of

the work was (and still is) that God might be magnified by the fact that the orphans under my care are provided with all they need only by prayer and faith, without any one being asked by me or my fellow labourers, whereby it may be seen that God is faithful still, and hears prayer still.[5]

Two weeks of prayer followed. On December 5, Müller, reading Psalm 81, felt confident that God was leading him forward. He wrote in his journal:

This evening, I was struck, in reading the Scriptures, with these words: "Open thy mouth wide, and I will fill it." I was led to apply this scripture to the orphan house, and asked the Lord for premises, one thousand pounds, and suitable individuals to take care of the children.[6]

Two days later, he received the first donation for the orphanage.

On April 11, 1836, Müller accepted the first children into the orphanage. Soon the orphanage reached full capacity, and the Lord provided funds for more buildings. If Oliver Twist had not been fictional, he could have found refuge in Müller's orphanage.

Years passed and the orphanage expanded, yet God provided even though Müller did not advertise the needs of the orphans. His journals relate account after account of God's unmistakable provision. Müller attested, "My Lord is not limited. He knows my present situation, and He can supply all I need."[7]

On December 9, 1859, Müller wrote,

Today it is twenty-four years since the orphan work commenced. What has God wrought! There have been received since then altogether 1,129 orphans, and during the last two years and two months alone 469, so greatly has the work increased of late. We have now 700 orphans under our care.[8]

God not only supplied for Müller and the orphans, but He also provided funds to give to God's work abroad. Müller found Hudson Taylor and the China Inland Mission to be quite like-minded. Taylor himself followed similar fund-raising principles to Müller's. Taylor expressed the same faith, famously stating, "God's work done in God's way will never lack God's supplies."[9]

One way God supplied for Taylor and his work was through Müller who became a trusted adviser and "a principle channel of support to the China Inland Mission."[10] Hudson Taylor received the following note from his general secretary in England: "Mr. Müller, after due consideration, has requested the names of all the brethren and sisters connected with the C.I.M., as he thinks it well to send help as he is able to each one." Mrs. Howard Taylor records that

> Mr. Müller's gifts for the next few years amounted to nearly £2000 annually [approximately $300,000 today]. In 1870, he sent Mr. Taylor £1940. He was now largely assisting twenty-one missionaries, who with twelve wives constituted the entire staff of the Mission, including Mr. and Mrs. Taylor.[11]

These gifts and many more continued in support of the work in China.

Even during Müller's lifetime, believers would protest that they could not trust God like Müller did. However, his primary motivation for opening the orphanage was to prove that God could provide. He argued that he did not have some special gift of faith. Müller wrote,

> Do not think that these answers to prayer are only for us and cannot be enjoyed by all the saints. Every child of God is not called by the Lord to establish schools and orphan houses and to trust in the Lord for means for them. Yet, there is no reason why you may not

experience, far more abundantly than we do now, His willingness to answer the prayers of His children.[12]

Later, he continued,

My faith is the same faith which is found in every believer. It has been increasing little by little for the last twenty-six years. Many times when I could have gone insane from worry, I was in peace because my soul believed the truth of that promise—"We know that all things work together for good to them that love God" (Romans 8:28).[13]

Müller rested on the promises of God. Throughout Scripture, God repeatedly promises to provide for His people. David testifies in Psalm 37:25, "I have been young, and now am old; yet have I not seen the righteous forsaken, nor his seed begging bread." Paul praises the Philippian believers for their generous giving to God's work and encourages them with the promise that "my God shall supply all your need according to his riches in glory by Christ Jesus" (Philippians 4:19). Jesus Himself commands His people not to worry about daily needs like food and clothing but instead to "seek ye first the kingdom of God, and his righteousness; and all these things shall be added unto you" (Matthew 6:33).

Müller's life provides an inspiring, historical example of living by faith. However, Scripture does not command Christians to live out their faith exactly as Müller did. God's Word neither requires believers to forfeit salaries nor forbids solicitation of funds for ministry. In 2 Corinthians 9, the apostle Paul asked for monetary gifts. We need not adopt all of Müller's methods, but we should absolutely emulate his faith!

Our trust should be in God, not money. If we have time to work overtime but no time to spend with God, we betray what we truly value. When fear of lacking what we need keeps us from being spiritual leaders at home and deprives us from doing what is eternally important, our most urgent lack is not physical but spiritual.

PERSONAL REFLECTION

- If I really believed God's promise to provide, how would it affect my decisions regarding employment, work hours, giving, and retirement?

- Is a perceived lack of funds holding me back from obeying God?

- Is the fear of losing what I have or could potentially earn keeping me from following God?

- How can I practically prioritize God and His kingdom over ambition, salary, and prestige?

FURTHER READING   **Matthew 6:19–34**

Müller, George. *The Autobiography of George Müller*. New Kensington, PA: Whitaker House, 1984.

Steer, Roger. *George Müller: Delighted in God. History Maker.* Wheaton, IL: Harold Shaw Publishers, 1981.

DAY 15

———— ◄ ————

ATTEMPT GREAT THINGS

"Expect great things from God; attempt great things for God."
—WILLIAM CAREY, MISSIONARY TO INDIA (1761–1834)

*"Enlarge the place of thy tent, and let them stretch forth the
curtains of thine habitations: spare not, lengthen thy cords, and
strengthen thy stakes; For thou shalt break forth on the right
hand and on the left; and thy seed shall inherit the Gentiles,
and make the desolate cities to be inhabited."*
—ISAIAH 54:2–3

The raging French Revolution stole the headlines in 1792, but a sermon in a small meeting in the hamlet of Nottingham, England, sparked a movement that would continue long beyond the crash of the last guillotine. William Carey challenged a fellowship of seventeen preachers to "expect great things from God; attempt great things for God." His text was Isaiah 54:2–3.

At age thirty-one, Carey was unknown beyond the small cluster of dissenting churches in the rural heart of England. Though he had been preaching for eight years, he had only been formally ordained to the pastorate the year before his famous sermon. Short and bald, his physical appearance impressed no one. Carey looked the part of his former profession, a humble shoemaker.

Though only God can see a man's heart, those around Carey saw the transformation of his life. Brought to a saving knowledge of Christ by a fellow apprentice in 1779, Carey joined his coworker in leading their nominal Christian master to genuine faith in Christ.[1] Not long thereafter, William won his two sisters, Mary and Ann, to Christ.[2]

Carey's burden for souls extended beyond his immediate surroundings. His evangelistic fervor intersected with his love for the Word of God and geography. In 1783, near the end of the American War for Independence, Carey borrowed the recent publication of *Captain Cook's Voyages*. Soon he fashioned a leather globe for his home and hand drew a map for the wall of his workshop. He researched statistics for Christianity in each region and wrote the figures on the map. His passion for the unreached began to be known.

Carey read the Great Commission and asked questions his contemporaries had not thought to ask. If churches baptized believers, should they not also disciple all nations? The two commands lay within the same commission (Matthew 28:19–20)!

In 1787, during his probationary period before formal ordination, Carey attended his first meeting of the Northampton Association, a preachers' fellowship not associated with the Church of England. The more seasoned pastors requested that new members introduce a theme for discussion. Carey proposed that they discuss "whether the command given to the apostles to teach all nations was not binding on all succeeding ministers to the end of the world seeing that the accompanying promise was of equal extent." A stinging rebuke dismissed his proposal: "Young man, sit down, sit down! You're an enthusiast. When God pleases to convert the heathen, He'll do it without consulting you or me."[3]

Unshaken by the opposition, Carey's passion for the unreached grew. The testimony of John Eliot and David Brainerd, missionaries to the Native Americans, inspired Carey. The example of the Moravians and Methodists challenged him. Should not the Baptists of England send out missionaries? Further influenced both by his growing understanding of God's Word and Captain Cook's descriptions of faraway places and peoples, Carey started to dream of taking the gospel to Tahiti.[4]

In 1788, Carey met Thomas Potts, an evangelistic businessman who had traveled in America. Seeing Carey's fervor for the gospel, Potts encouraged Carey to write a pamphlet urging worldwide evangelization. If Carey wrote it, Potts would finance its printing.[5] With the blessing of his preacher's fellowship, in May 1792 Carey published his eighty-seven-page pamphlet, *An Inquiry into the Obligation of Christians to Use Means for the Conversion of the Heathen*. This laid the foundation for his famous sermon less than a month later.

According to his biographer and great-grandson, S. Pearce Carey, William Carey began his message by putting Isaiah 54 into its historical context. Judah would be destroyed and carried into captivity, but God would keep His promises to His people. The Jews should expect God to do great things for them. They should anticipate His working on their behalf, bringing them back from captivity and reinhabiting the abandoned cities of Israel.[6] Based on this expectation, God's people should act in faith on God's promise. They should enlarge their tents using broader canvas, taller poles, and thicker stakes, preparing for the promised increase.[7] They should attempt great things for God.

Carey compared God's challenge to Judah to His commission to the church. The dissenting Baptists, like Judah, struggled and failed. They were weak, but the promises of God were not weak. God's people must expect God to keep His Word, and therefore, attempt great things for God. By great things, Carey meant the Great Commission—the evangelization of the lost around the world.

The very next day, the fellowship founded the Baptist Society for Propagating the Gospel among the Heathens. Carey himself would be the first contributor, pledging all the earnings from the sale of the pamphlet. Not long thereafter, he would also become the society's first missionary—not to Tahiti, but to India.

God would use William Carey and the society he helped found to attempt and achieve great things for God. For forty-one years, Carey would faithfully plod for God in India, establishing a primary school for both boys and girls and a Bible college. He also translated the Bible into Bengali, Hindi, Sanskrit, Oriya, Marathi, and Assamese. His work in India and influence around the world resulted in William Carey becoming known as "The Father of Modern Missions."

Do I expect great things from God? Do I bank on His promises? Do I anticipate that God will do what He says He will do and so act accordingly? Do I expect God to do the impossible?

We only see God do the impossible when we attempt the impossible. We attempt the impossible when we root our expectations on the promises of God.

Enlarge your tent. Dream Word-inspired dreams. Envision what can be done, not what cannot. See opportunities where others see obstacles. Strike the word *impossible* from your vocabulary. Attempt great things as you rely on a great God.

PERSONAL REFLECTION

- How are my attempts to serve God limited by my small expectations of what God could do in me and through me?

- How can I better base my expectations on what God has promised in His Word?

- If I do not expect God to work as He has promised, who then do I believe is ultimately in control of this world?

FURTHER READING   **Isaiah 54**

Carey, S. Pearce. *William Carey*. London: Carey Press, 1934.

DAY 16

————— ◄ —————

IN THE PRESENCE
OF THE ALMIGHTY

*"I have cast myself into the hands of Almighty God,
who reigns everywhere."*

—PATRICK OF IRELAND (5ᵀᴴ CENTURY)

*"Call upon me in the day of trouble:
I will deliver thee, and thou shalt glorify me."*

—PSALM 50:15

Crack! The heavy wooden door surrendered to the fierce blows of the marauders. Sixteen-year-old Patrick, aroused from sleep, had nowhere to run. Red-haired Irishmen seized him, bound his hands, and dragged him out of his home in Britain and across the Irish Sea. When Patrick's wealthy parents returned from their travels, they had little hope they would ever see their kidnapped son again.[1]

For the next six years, Patrick toiled as a slave, keeping sheep. On the rolling hills of Ireland, the gospel, taught to him in his childhood, came back to his memory. God used the trials of his captivity to turn his heart toward Christ for salvation.

One day, Patrick attempted a daring escape from his masters. He fled from the pastures for the sea. Desperate to go anywhere away from Ireland, Patrick boarded a pirate ship for the continent.

Ancient France, in a period of turmoil, proved to be a wilderness. Yet, God provided food for his journey, strengthening his faith. After six years as a captive and a harrowing journey, prolonged by lengthy detours, Patrick finally returned to his parents in Britain.

His family vainly hoped that after his against-all-odds return, Patrick would remain with them, but he increasingly felt the call of God to return to Ireland. This time, he would go, not as a slave, but as a missionary. Later, he would record his reasoning for going, quoting from the Great Commission passages of the New Testament:

> The Lord teaches and admonishes in the Gospel, saying: "Going, therefore, teach ye all nations, baptizing them in the name of the Father and of the Son and of the Holy Ghost, even to the consummation of the world." And again: "Go ye into the whole world, and preach the Gospel to every creature."[2]

He further explains,

> Whence did I obtain afterwards the great and salutary gift to know or love God, and to leave my country and my relations, although many gifts were offered to me with sorrow and tears. And I offended many of my seniors then against my will. But, guided by God, I yielded in no way to them—not to me, but to God be the glory, who conquered in me, and resisted them all; so that I came to the Irish people to preach the Gospel, and bear with the injuries of the unbelieving, and listen to the reproach of being a stranger, and endure many persecutions, even to chains, and to give up my freedom for the benefit of others. And if I be worthy, I am ready to give up my life unhesitat-

ingly and most cheerfully for His name, and thus, if the Lord permit,
I desire to spend it even until my death.[3]

As he served in the land of his former captors, Patrick felt the
risk. He wrote,

> For daily I expect to be murdered or betrayed or reduced to slavery
> if the occasion arises. But I fear nothing, because of the promises of
> Heaven; for I have cast myself into the hands of Almighty God, who
> reigns everywhere. As the prophet says: Cast your burden on the
> Lord and he will sustain you.[4]

To the end of his life, Patrick served in Ireland, leading hundreds
to Christ.

Whether his lot be as a slave, a journeyman, or a missionary
to a hostile nation, Patrick keenly felt the presence of Christ. The
following poem, an excerpt from a larger work, is attributed to
this apostle to Ireland. In it, Patrick expresses his awareness of
Christ's imminence in his daily life:

> Christ with me,
> Christ before me,
> Christ behind me,
> Christ in me,
> Christ beneath me,
> Christ above me,
> Christ on my right,
> Christ on my left,
> Christ when I lie down,
> Christ when I sit down,
> Christ when I arise,
> Christ in the heart of every man who thinks of me,
> Christ in the mouth of everyone who speaks of me,
> Christ in every eye that sees me,
> Christ in every ear that hears me.[5]

Much of Patrick's life lies in obscurity. Often the writings attributed to him seem vague or allegorical. However, through the sixteen centuries since his death, a few clear points shine through. First, Patrick believed in the importance of the gospel, leaving his home to spread it among his enemies. This early Celtic believer obeyed the Great Commission over a thousand years before William Carey left for India. Second, Patrick knew Scripture and took it seriously. His testimony in *The Confessions of St. Patrick* overflows with quotes and references to the Word of God. Third, Patrick trusted the promises of God. He knew Christ would never leave him. He cast his burden on the Lord in his day of trouble. When God delivered, Patrick made it his life's mission to magnify his God. He lived the promise of Psalm 50:15: "Call upon me in the day of trouble: I will deliver thee, and thou shalt glorify me."

In our "day of trouble," to whom do we turn? Many turn to themselves, relying on past experience, innate talent, personal discipline, or careful planning. Some turn to others—family, friends, or coworkers. Others just give up. Few turn to God first.

Where do I go when life is coming apart? Do I trust in the presence of Christ who is with me, before me, behind me, in me, beneath me, above me, on my right, on my left, where I lie down, where I sit down, and where I stand up?

When God delivers, whether I trusted Him or not, do I give Him the glory? Do I make sure that others know what God has done for me? Our praise for God should begin with our salvation and spread across all aspects of our lives. Those near us should come to expect us to share how God intervenes in our lives, delivering, providing, guiding, and sustaining.

Our awareness of Christ's presence should unmistakably overflow unto others. Not only should others hear us acknowledge Christ with our mouths, but they should also see Him in our lives. Is Christ in the mind of every man who thinks of me? Is He in the mouth of everyone who speaks of me? Is Christ in every eye that sees me and in every ear that hears me?

PERSONAL REFLECTION

- How is the presence of Christ seen in my daily life?
- If I truly believe that Christ is with me all the time and everywhere, how would this embolden me?
- When I face trouble, to whom do I turn first? God? Family? Friends? Teachers? Coworkers?

FURTHER READING   Joshua 1:1–9

Haykin, Michael A. G. *Patrick of Ireland: His Life and Impact.* Greanies House, UK: Christian Focus, 2014.

DAY 17

---◀---

BE BOLD

"Christ is with us until the world's end.
Let his little flock be bold therefore."[1]

—WILLIAM TYNDALE, BIBLE TRANSLATOR (1494–1536)

"And I say unto you my friends, Be not afraid of them that kill
the body, and after that have no more that they can do. But I
will forewarn you whom ye shall fear: Fear him, which after
he hath killed hath power to cast into hell; yea, I say unto you,
Fear him. Are not five sparrows sold for two farthings, and not
one of them is forgotten before God? But even the very hairs of
your head are all numbered. Fear not therefore:
ye are of more value than many sparrows."

—LUKE 12:4–7

Y ou go first," said William Tyndale, politely standing aside for his younger friend. They were headed to a restaurant in Antwerp, Belgium, on a damp evening in May of 1535.

"No, I insist," Henry Phillips protested, leaving the narrow path between the buildings for his new mentor.

Tyndale relented and stepped into the alley. Two burly men, materializing out of the shadows, rushed toward Tyndale. The forty-one-year-old scholar turned back, but Phillips blocked his path. His cunning new friend had betrayed him. For the next 500 days, Tyndale shivered in the darkness of the towering Vilvoorde prison.

Thirteen years before, soon after he graduated from Oxford, Tyndale had come to the conviction that every common man in England needed to read the Word of God for himself in his mother tongue. Martin Luther had just published the New Testament in German in 1522, and Tyndale owned a copy of the Greek text Erasmus had recently compiled in 1516. God had provided Tyndale both the example and the tools to translate the Bible from the original languages into English for the first time.

Though employed as a private tutor in a wealthy home, Tyndale seized opportunities to preach the Word in nearby villages. He proclaimed Scripture rather than the dogma of the Roman Catholic Church, using English rather than Latin so that the common people would understand. The vicar general of the region considered Tydale's preaching to be heresy and summoned the young preacher for a stern rebuke. The state religion's opposition to Tyndale's work of spreading the truth had begun.

Not long afterward, during a dinner discussion with local Roman Catholic clergy, Tyndale declared, "If God spare my life ere many years, I will cause a boy that driveth the plow, shall know more of the Scripture than thou dost."[2] Over the next two years, Tyndale labored on his English translation of the New Testament. When the ecclesiastical authorities refused him official permission to publish it, Tyndale decided to continue his work on the European continent, free of the growing opposition in England. He would never again return to his homeland.

DAY 17 | WILLIAM TYNDALE

For the next eleven years, Tyndale haunted the printing districts of Germany and the Low Countries (modern-day Netherlands and Belgium). He became adept at concealing himself and his work from those who opposed the English translation of the Bible. Like-minded scholars, sympathetic merchants, and profit-loving printers aided his efforts to publish the New Testament, followed by a steady stream of his own theological works. The Roman Catholic Church and its allies in England banned all his writings, but the books and pamphlets made their way into circulation nonetheless. Despite his growing influence, Tyndale knew his time was limited.

Never knowing when the hammer would fall, Tyndale put his trust in the promises of God. This became a major theme of his writings. In 1848, a few centuries after Tyndale's death, his known works were compiled into one book. In this volume, the word *promise* appears 481 times.

In 1528, Tyndale wrote *The Obedience of a Christian Man*. Besides his translation of the Bible, this work would become his most popular book—read even by King Henry VIII himself. In this work, Tyndale confessed his faith in the promises of God, explaining,

> He [God] hath sworn; he is true; he will fulfill the promises that he hath made unto Abraham, Isaac, and Jacob. This is written for our learning: for verily he is a true God; and is our God as well as theirs; and his promises are with us, as well as with them; and he present with us, as well as he was with them. If we ask, we shall obtain; if we knock, he will open; if we seek, we shall find. . . . Christ is with us until the world's end. Let his little flock be bold therefore. For if God be on our side, what matter maketh it who be against us, be they bishops, cardinals, popes, or whatsoever names they will?[3]

These were no idle words. As Tyndale translated the promises of God and exhorted those who followed Scripture to be bold for God, he anticipated that he himself would likely put these very same promises to the test. He had seen some of his closest friends endangered by association with him. Even a common Englishman who had never seen the author could be arrested for merely owning Tyndale's writings.

In 1533, John Frith, a young scholar and Tyndale's disciple, ignored his mentor's warnings about returning to England. Soon, because of his association with Tyndale and his own bold words against Roman Catholic teaching, Frith sat in jail awaiting his inevitable fate. During this time, Tyndale wrote two Scripture-filled letters to encourage Frith to be faithful, reminding him of the promises of God: "There falleth not a hair till His hour be come: and when His hour is come, necessity carrieth us hence, though we be not willing."[4] Frith's time came. Three years before his mentor suffered the same fate, Frith's enemies tied him to a wooden stake and burned him to death for his beliefs.

As we today consider the life of William Tyndale, we might ask why he had to die. Given the religious and political atmosphere of his times, maybe a better question would be, "How did Tyndale survive so long?" From 1522 to 1524, God protected Tyndale in England despite his audacity to begin translating the New Testament. Then for eleven more years on the continent, God held back the wrath of the ecclesiastical authorities. Tyndale had time to finish translating the New Testament and complete much of the Old Testament, publish multiple editions, and produce at least six of his own original works. His writings caught the attention of the leading English minds of his day. They inspired men and women across England to follow Scripture, even at the risk of their lives.

Each life is a candle. Every candle is a different length. No one knows how long his candle is. Until your candle burns to nothing, let your light shine with white-hot brilliance.

Tyndale wrote, "Christ is our head; and God's word is that wherein our life resteth. To cleave, therefore, fast unto Christ, and unto those promises which God hath made us for his sake, is our wisdom."[5] Be as bold as Tyndale. Work as tirelessly in the work God has entrusted to you. Rest with peace in your heart on God's promises.

PERSONAL REFLECTION

- How bright is my candle? How am I lighting the darkness around me?

- Am I seeking a minimum-risk, maximum-comfort life? If I followed the commands and examples in Scripture, what risks should I be taking for the cause of Christ?

- In what areas of my life could I be bolder by relying on God's promises?

FURTHER READING   Acts 4

Daniell, David. *William Tyndale: A Biography.* New Haven, CT: Yale University Press, 1994.

DAY 18

NOTHING CAN STAND IN OUR WAY

"Nothing can stand in our way,
not even the demon they say lives in that hut."
—STANLEY DALE, MISSIONARY TO PAPUA, INDONESIA
(1916–1968)

"I will build my church; and the gates of hell
shall not prevail against it."
—MATTHEW 16:18

We will dismantle that spirit house on the knoll tomorrow," said Australian missionary Stan Dale in the spring of 1961. The local Yali tribesmen in the remote Papua Indonesian ravine understood none of the former World War II commando's words. Awed by the sheer audacity of the first white man they had ever seen, the warring villagers laid down their weapons. They agreed to peace, despite a neighboring village's murder of four of their women on the night of the seven foreigners' arrival. None of the warriors even moved as Stan tromped through their sacred spirit house and then condemned it to make way for a future airstrip. Dale had no idea that not long before, the tribesmen watching him had murdered a beloved toddler for trespassing on that very site. His coworker, the Dutchman Bruno deLeeuw, trembled at his friend's boldness, cautioning him to no avail. Now the two Caucasians and their five Christian Dani companions set to clear the hillside, including the spirit house.

In the Dani language, Dale encouraged the men with the promises of God:

> We have not come into this valley at the word of men, but at the command of our Lord Jesus Christ, who said, "Go into all the world and make disciples among all men!" He also said, "And lo, I am with you always, even to the end of the world!" That means He is with us in this very place, and nothing can stand in our way, not even the demon they say lives in that hut. . . . In fact, if that demon knows what's good for him, he'll be high-tailing it for some other valley before we even cross that stone wall! And then he translated into Dani the immortal promise of Jesus: "I will build my church, and the gates of hell will not prevail against it!" And that goes for hell's stone walls too![1]

Though Yali tribesmen, wearing little besides their weapons, watched and grumbled, Dale and DeLeeuw survived the building of the airstrip. God protected them by confusing those who would have killed and eaten them. Next, Dale and DeLeeuw built houses. Dale's family of seven moved into the ravine. From 1961 to 1968, they and other missionaries learned the Yali language and then began sharing the gospel.

The gates of hell could not withstand the advance of Christ's church. Young men responded, first in curiosity, and then in belief.

Then, as increasing numbers of both men and women came to Christ, these new Yali believers burnt their fetishes, fully rejecting the demon worship and superstition of their forefathers.

Such a bold advance provoked a violent reaction. Appalled by the transformation of their people and fearing retribution by the spirits, tribesmen from surrounding villages spread word that the teachers must be killed. On September 25, 1968, energized by the power of hell, they ambushed Dale and his coworker Phil Masters. Soon dozens of arrows pierced the missionaries' bodies.

The warriors reveled in their victory over the new teaching, but they celebrated too soon. Though he had died a martyr's death, Dale's words proved to be true. "Nothing can stand in our way." Nothing, not even his own death, could halt the advance of Christ's church.

The new Yali believers, emboldened by the sacrifice of their spiritual fathers, spread their new faith. One woman said, "In spite of all that has happened I believe that the Word of God will prevail. It cannot become as nothing, no matter what its enemies may do!"[2] Within four years, many of the men who murdered Dale and Masters, through an awe-inspiring story of God's providence, came to Christ.

Today, we forget the power of Christ's promises to His people. Most of us neither face the dangers nor enjoy the fruit that missionaries like Stan Dale did. We see a church that in many parts of the world looks weak. The host of dwindling assemblies in desperate need for revitalization overwhelms us. The fear of the unknown restrains us from striking out and planting new works where Bible-preaching churches do not exist. A sense of futility chokes our witness and snuffs out the light of the gospel under our bushel. We shrink back when we should surge forward. Could it be because we have forgotten the promises of God? Give us God-guided boldness!

The promises Dale lived are the same promises we can claim today. Few of us are former commandos, and that is probably a good thing. However, God can use us and our unique backgrounds to advance His church. The work of Christ's church is the responsibility of every believer, but the advance is up to God. He promises to build His church. We get the privilege to participate in this victorious work.

If we truly believe the promises of God, then we must step out in faith. Nothing can stop us because nothing can stop Him.

PERSONAL REFLECTION

- What steps could I take right now to advance the gospel?

- How can I live in a way that demonstrates that I truly believe God's light can overpower the darkness of this world?

- What promises from God's Word do I claim for support when I face opposition in my service to Christ?

FURTHER READING   **Matthew 16:13–27**

Richardson, Don. *Lords of the Earth: An Incredible but True Story from the Stone-Age Hell of Papua's Jungle.* Glendale, CA: Regal Books, 1977.

DAY 19

―――――― ◀ ――――――

SUFFERING
AND SUCCESS

*"It seems to be a law of the Kingdom that there is no success
without suffering. If you succeed without suffering it means
that someone suffered before you. If you suffer without succeeding, one who comes after you will doubtless have the success."*[1]
—EDWARD JUDSON, FORMER MISSIONARY KID (1844-1914)

*"And let us not be weary in well doing:
for in due season we shall reap, if we faint not."*
—GALATIANS 6:9

Edward Judson had no memories of his mother. On April 26,
1845, Edward, merely sixteen months old, remained under
the care of friends in Maulmain, Burma, with two of his siblings.
His mother, Sarah Boardman Judson, and his father, Adoniram
Judson, with Edward's three elder siblings boarded a ship for
New England. The family vainly hoped that a return home would
provide the rest needed for Sarah's recovery from a lingering illness. But long before they reached America, Adoniram buried

his second wife on the Isle of France, a lonely island off the coast of Madagascar.[2]

From an early age, Edward Judson understood suffering. He personally sacrificed much for the cross of Christ before he even became aware of who he was or why he spent his early years in Burma instead of the United States. Despite these hardships, Edward grew up to be a theology teacher and pastor in the United States. He also authored a biography of his famous father. In the foreword, Edward wrote the following dedication: "To the children of missionaries, the involuntary inheritors of their parents' sufferings and rewards, this book is affectionately dedicated by one of their number."[3]

When faithful men and women follow their Savior into a path of difficulty, they are not the only ones who sacrifice. Few think of the sacrifice of the children who grow up in a faraway land. Even fewer consider the cost inflicted on the grandparents who, by no choice of their own, forfeit the presence of both their children and their grandchildren.

When Edward's father, Adoniram, asked his first wife's father for her hand in marriage, Adoniram wrote the following devastatingly honest letter:

> I have now to ask whether you can consent to part with your daughter early next spring, to see her no more in this world? Whether you can consent to her departure to a heathen land, and her subjection to the hardships and sufferings of a missionary life? Whether you can consent to her exposure to the dangers of the ocean; to the fatal influence of the southern climate of India; to every kind of want and distress; to degradation, insult, persecution, and perhaps a violent death? Can you consent to all this, for the sake of Him who left His heavenly home and died for her and for you; for the sake of perish-

ing, immortal souls; for the sake of Zion and the glory of God? Can you consent to all this, in hope of soon meeting your daughter in the world of glory, with a crown of righteousness brightened by the acclamations of praise which shall redound to her Saviour from heathens saved, through her means, from eternal woe and despair?[4]

In an astounding act of faith, her father consented and made the sacrifice. His daughter would pass away nearly sixteen years later in service of her Lord in Burma.

When such a sacrifice is made, the cost can feel too great. If there is no immediate fruit from the sacrifice, those reeling from the loss can question whether their sacrifice was in vain. Our hearts can rise up, feeling robbed by the injustice of this world, and we can begin to question God's sovereignty.

When facing such emotions, we must rest on the promises of God. What bereaved parents sowed in their children, they will reap in eternal rewards. Their weeping can turn to tears of joy when they consider, as Edward Judson pointed out in his preface, both the sufferings and the rewards of missionary service.

In Psalm 126, as Israel endured the Babylonian captivity, the Lord encouraged Israel to keep serving Him through their suffering. God promised, "They that sow in tears shall reap in joy. He that goeth forth and weepeth, bearing precious seed, shall doubtless come again with rejoicing, bringing his sheaves with him" (Psalm 126:5-6). Not every Israelite lived to join the reaping. Many died before the captivity finished. However, the harvest came as God promised.

In the New Testament, Paul repeats God's promise in Galatians 6:7-9:

Be not deceived; God is not mocked: for whatsoever a man soweth, that shall he also reap. For he that soweth to his flesh shall of the flesh reap corruption; but he that soweth to the Spirit shall of the Spirit reap life everlasting. And let us not be weary in well doing: for in due season we shall reap, if we faint not.

That which is sown to the Spirit—like the loss of family in the work of God—will bear everlasting results. Christ Himself speaks of the harvest in John 4:35–38:

> Say not ye, There are yet four months, and then cometh harvest? behold, I say unto you, Lift up your eyes, and look on the fields; for they are white already to harvest. And he that reapeth receiveth wages, and gathereth fruit unto life eternal: that both he that soweth and he that reapeth may rejoice together. And herein is that saying true, One soweth, and another reapeth. I sent you to reap that whereon ye bestowed no labour: other men laboured, and ye are entered into their labours.

Remembering his family's experiences from hardships to harvest, Edward Judson said, "There is no success without suffering. If you succeed without suffering it means that someone suffered before you. If you suffer without succeeding; one who comes after you will doubtless have the success."[5] Those who followed Adoniram Judson to Burma reaped in the harvest what the pioneer missionary sowed at great cost. Thousands of people across Burma came to Christ.

Today, we, too, stand on the shoulders of faithful men and women who have gone before us. All success in ministry is a work of God. Beyond this, much fruit we see personally is also a direct result of those who paved the way for our ministries. Many of them saw little fruit, but we today see it, reaping where they have sown. In the twenty-first century, there are few, genuine pioneer ministries across the world. We build on the foundation left by previous generations.

PERSONAL REFLECTION

- What am I sowing today? What will I do if nothing seems to sprout?

- Will I sustain my efforts to witness to my relatives and neighbors even if they show no interest for decades?

- Will I persevere in bringing up my children in the nurture and admonition of the Lord even when their spiritual growth seems stunted?

- When results come, does God get the glory? Do I share the credit with those who labored with me and before me?

FURTHER READING **John 4:1–42**

DAY 20

---◀---

SURRENDER

"It's complete surrender."

—ERIC LIDDELL, MISSIONARY TO CHINA (1902–1945)

*"I beseech you therefore, brethren, by the mercies of God, that
ye present your bodies a living sacrifice, holy, acceptable unto
God, which is your reasonable service. And be not conformed
to this world: but be ye transformed by the renewing of your
mind, that ye may prove what is that good, and acceptable,
and perfect, will of God."*

—ROMANS 12:1–2

It's complete surrender," said forty-three-year-old Eric Liddell
as he slipped into a coma. A brain tumor ended his two-year
confinement in a Japanese internment camp in northern China.[1]
These last words highlight a major theme throughout Liddell's
life and writings.

Eric Liddell surrendered to Christ as a young man. For Liddell,
surrender meant putting God first in everything, even if it meant
the ridicule of the United Kingdom for not running an Olympic
race on Sunday. Surrender meant starting each day alone with
God, whether in an idyllic, pastoral landscape in Scotland or in the

squalor of an overcrowded internment camp in China. Surrender meant consistent godly living even when deprivations made other detainees, including some missionaries, behave like barbarians.

From his youth through adulthood, Liddell consistently encouraged fellow believers to cultivate a habit of daily yieldedness to Christ. He told them:

> Victory over all the circumstances of life comes not by might, nor by power, but by a practical confidence in God and by allowing His Spirit to dwell in our hearts and control our actions and emotions. Learn in the days of ease and comfort . . . so that when the days of hardship come you will be fully prepared and equipped to meet them."[2]

He wrote these words from his experience in the tense years leading up to World War II in Japanese-occupied China.

Just before his imprisonment, Liddell finished writing a year-long, month-by-month discipleship manual for new believers, designed to aid them in Christian growth. A major emphasis of this work was surrender. Liddell wrote,

> Obedience to God's will is the secret of spiritual knowledge and insight. . . . Let us put ourselves before ourselves and look at ourselves. The bravest moment in a man's life is the moment he looks at himself objectively without wincing, without complaining. Self-examination which does not result in action is dangerous. What am I going to do about what I see? The action called for is surrender to God.[3]

Liddell lived out his surrender to God. In 1925, he gave up his Olympic racing career for missions work in China. After two years teaching science in a missionary school in China, Eric exchanged this comparatively comfortable post for itinerant, evangelistic work in the war-ravaged Hebei province. As tensions mounted, he sacrificed time with his family, sending them to safety across the sea as he stayed to aid those in danger. Liddell practiced what he preached. He lived a life of surrender.

Surrender and obedience pave the way for knowing and proving God's will. Liddell wrote, "God's will is only revealed to us step by step. He reveals more as we obey what we know. Surrender means that we are prepared to follow his will step by step as it is revealed to us, no matter what the cost."[4] He continues in another section of his book, "Obedience to God's will is the secret of spiritual knowledge and insight. It is not willingness to know, but willingness to do (obey) God's will that brings certainty."[5]

Liddell's words sound quite similar to the promise of God in Romans 12:1–2:

> I beseech you therefore, brethren, by the mercies of God, that ye present your bodies a living sacrifice, holy, acceptable unto God, which is your reasonable service. And be not conformed to this world: but be ye transformed by the renewing of your mind, that ye may prove what is that good, and acceptable, and perfect, will of God.

How does a believer find the will of God? He must surrender his life as a living sacrifice, obediently separate from the world, and constantly renew his mind with the Word of God. Note the logic of Romans 12:1–2. There is no sacrifice without surrender, and there is no surrender without rejecting conformity to the world and living in obedience to Christ. Furthermore, there is no strength for obedience without ongoing renewal. Liddell wrote, "Surrender means the end of the great rebellion of our wills."[6] Only when we give up our own will can we truly discern what is God's will.

Am I living the surrendered life? If I'm not sure, then I'm not. Surrender is a conscious decision.

This decision begins with presenting my body a living sacrifice. I must wholeheartedly pray, "Lord, as long as I am in this body and on this earth, I am yours. Use me."

Surrender continues with daily commitment to God. Liddell challenges new believers to ask themselves: "Have I surrendered this new day to God, and will I seek and obey the guidance of the Holy Spirit throughout its hours?"[7] We should live in the spirit of this prayer: "Lord, I am Yours today. I want to do what You want me to do. Show me where my will clashes with Yours, and I will submit. Use me today."

Surrender puts Christ on the throne of my life, but so often I snatch His crown and wield His scepter. The surrendered life is a life of unyieldingly resisting the Devil and my own selfish lusts, and constantly submitting to God. I know my weakness and so seek His strength to do His will.

God calls every believer to live the surrendered life. God reveals His will to those who have already decided to do it. What have I decided?

PERSONAL REFLECTION

- Am I living the surrendered life today? Why or why not?
- Did I once live the surrendered life but now no longer do? How do I sustain the surrendered life?
- Am I soft, moldable clay in the hands of the Potter, or am I a stubborn lump, refusing the shape of the vessel He seeks to make with my life?

FURTHER READING **Romans 12**

Hamilton, Duncan. *For the Glory: The Untold and Inspiring Story of Eric Liddell, Hero of Chariots of Fire.* New York: Penguin House, 2016.

DAY 21

GOD'S WILL

"I pray Thee blend my human will with Thine."
**—AMY CARMICHAEL, MISSIONARY TO JAPAN AND INDIA
(1867–1951)**

*"I will instruct thee and teach thee in the way which
thou shalt go: I will guide thee with mine eye."*
—PSALM 32:8

Go ye!" For four years, the words of the Great Commission
had pulled at Amy Carmichael's heart. Finally, on January
13, 1892, she decided she must go. But where?

China? Having heard Hudson Taylor's impassioned pleas for the
millions there dying without Christ, Amy applied to his organization,
the China Inland Mission. They rejected her for health reasons.

Japan? Exactly one year after her decision to go into missions,
Carmichael recorded that "the thought came" to go to Japan. She
described it as a "strange feeling" that she should leave as soon as
possible. Having written to Barclay Buxton, the leader of the field
in Japan, she boarded a ship for Asia without waiting for a reply
of acceptance.[1]

Sri Lanka? Carmichael's next move came suddenly. For just over a year after her arrival in Japan, Carmichael struggled to learn the Japanese language. Then she contracted a mysterious ailment diagnosed as "Japanese head" or "brain exhaustion." The doctors recommended a change of climate. On July 10, 1894, Carmichael arrived in Shanghai, intending to return to Japan after regaining her strength. By July 18, her plans had changed completely. She wrote, "The word of the Lord came unto me saying 'Go to Ceylon'" (modern-day Sri Lanka). How she heard this, no one then or now knows. Neither the missionaries who hosted her in China, nor her teammates back in Japan, nor her supporters in England understood her sudden change of direction. She would soon write from Sri Lanka concerning her abrupt decision and lack of communication: "I see my wrongness and cannot be sorry enough."[2]

India? Carmichael's time in Sri Lanka lasted only a few months. The elderly Englishman who was like a father to her had a stroke, and she rushed home to nurse him to health. A year later, in 1895, Carmichael walked through a new open door. Accepted by a different mission society, she headed for Bangalore. Carmichael would serve in India without furlough for the next fifty-five years.

Finding her place in the Lord's work proved to be a challenge for Amy Carmichael. Even in India, God changed her course. Determined to pursue itinerant evangelism in villages across southern India, Carmichael found it hard to surrender this work as God brought the need of temple children and other neglected youths into her life. Yet, she did relent, and God gave her a fruitful ministry with these children—raising them, leading them to Christ, and discipling them.

Decades later, Carmichael would share how she learned to follow God's leading:

> The devil sometimes speaks and tries to deceive us into thinking it is the voice of God. He tries to get us, who long to walk in the light, to follow instead a will-o-the-wisp into the marsh. In the matter of guidance there are three important points: 1. The Word of the Lord in the Bible. 2. The Word of the Spirit in our heart. 3. The circumstances of our lives, which have been arranged by God.[3]

Though she had begun to follow these principles early in her missionary career, Carmichael's initial path seems at times to have been destabilized by will-o-the-wisp moments. However, these three guidelines provide an excellent starting point in seeking God's will. We might ask for a further explanation of her second criterion. We may protest that seeking godly counsel should be added to her list. However, we can learn much from Carmichael's early experiences as she learned to seek God's will.

As we in the twenty-first century look back on a single, Victorian woman taking the gospel to a developing India, we might be tempted to look down on her early struggles to find the will of God. Modern readers with anachronistic prejudice may also find fault with how Amy Carmichael handled the complex, cross-cultural issues of her times. They might criticize how she oversaw her groundbreaking work among the downtrodden of India.

However, Carmichael's heart for knowing God, following His leading, and serving Him wholeheartedly are worthy of emulation. Her transparency—both about her struggles in the work and about the realities of bringing light into a dark world—has done the church a great service. Her example of humble service supported her words. She exhorted her coworkers in the orphanage, "Be the first . . . wherever there is a sacrifice to be made, a self-denial to be practiced, or an impetus to be given."[4] She did not ask them to do anything she had not already done herself.

Like this dedicated woman of the past, we should pray:

And shall I pray Thee change Thy will, My Father,
Until it be according unto mine?
But, no, Lord, no, that never shall be, rather
I pray Thee blend my human will with Thine.[5]

Is this my prayer? Am I seeking for God to guide me? Am I willing to go wherever He leads?

Throughout Scripture, God promises to lead and guide the humble. In Psalm 25:9, He pledges, "The meek will he guide in judgment: and the meek will he teach his way." In Psalm 32:8, God states, "I will instruct thee and teach thee in the way which thou shalt go: I will guide thee with mine eye." In Proverbs 3:5–6, He says, "Trust in the LORD with all thine heart; and lean not unto thine own understanding. In all thy ways acknowledge him, and he shall direct thy paths." In Psalm 37:23–24, God promises, "The steps of a good man are ordered by the LORD: and he delighteth in his way. Though he fall, he shall not be utterly cast down: for the LORD upholdeth him with his hand."

Do I claim these promises from God's Word in my own life? Do I trust God to lead me? Do I look for His hand in the circumstances of life?

Do I with Amy Carmichael and the psalmist pray, "I delight to do thy will, O my God: yea, thy law is within my heart" (Psalm 40:8)? Do I implore God, "Lead me, O LORD, in thy righteousness. . . . make thy way straight before my face" (Psalm 5:8)? Have

I asked God to give me the desires of my heart—to make me want what He wants me to want (Psalm 37:4)? Have I implored God that I "might be filled with the knowledge of his will in all wisdom and spiritual understanding" (Colossians 1:9)? Does my heart yearn for God to "make [me] perfect in every good work to do his will, working in [me] that which is wellpleasing in his sight" (Hebrews 13:21)? When I pray the Lord's Prayer, do I truly mean, "Thy will be done in earth, as it is in heaven" (Matthew 6:10)? Have I surrendered like Christ in Gethsemane, saying, "Not my will, but thine be done" (Luke 22:42)?

Is my will blended with His as much as a fallen will can be?

PERSONAL REFLECTION

- What do I want the most in life?

- How do my desires compare with what the Bible says are God's desires for me? Are there any desires in my heart that clash with God's desires for me for which I should repent?

- How can I cultivate the right desires within my heart? What steps can I take to submit my desires to God's will?

FURTHER READING   **Psalm 37**

Elliot, Elisabeth. *A Chance to Die: The Life and Legacy of Amy Carmichael*. Old Tappan, NJ: Fleming H. Revell Company, 1987.

Carmichael, Amy. *Things as They Are: Mission Work in Southern India*. London: Morgan and Scott, 1905.

RESULTS

"Christ sent me to preach the Gospel,
and He will look after the results."

—MARY SLESSOR, MISSIONARY TO NIGERIA (1848–1915)

"I have planted, Apollos watered; but God gave the increase."

—1 CORINTHIANS 3:6

Run, Ma!" the Nigerian women caring for the orphans shouted, rousing the Scottish missionary from her sleep. Already dressed and packed, Mary Slessor ran, not fleeing in terror from the inevitable conflict but charging directly toward the rampaging warriors. This scene was often repeated during Slessor's time in the Okoyong district of Nigeria. On one such occasion in 1890, Slessor's daring dash particularly concerned her friends. As if the long run through the African jungle were not danger enough, Mary knew she was headed toward a band of notoriously violent men, frenzied with alcohol and worked up for revenge.

"I have heard of no war," the chief of the village said when Mary arrived, breathless and spent. He did not want her to interfere. If there was a war, the chief declared, "[they were] not likely to be helped by a woman."

"In measuring the woman's power," she responded, "you have evidently forgotten to take into account the woman's God."[1]

What audacity! What woman would dare to challenge tribal chiefs of Nigeria in such a fashion? Who was this woman who would calmly knit as warriors, draped with weapons, would argue and threaten each other for hours only to submit to her decision at the end of the conference? Who was this woman who would oppose the centuries-old belief that twins were devils deserving death, snatching them from parents bent on murdering them? Who was this woman who rescued babies, defended battered women, and sheltered abused slaves, providing refuge in her own mud hut from those who pursued them?

In her nearly fifty-year ministry in the Calabar region of Nigeria, Mary Slessor would tame an entire district. She would be a driving force in changing a culture of violence to a culture of commerce. Her contributions to bringing peace to this tribal area of Nigeria would earn her accolades during her lifetime. After her death, her face would for a time grace the ten-pound Scottish note! Who was this woman?

An attendee at one of her meetings during a furlough in Scotland in 1898 described her:

> She was a most gentle-looking lady . . . rather below the average height, a complexion like yellow parchment, and short lank brown hair: a most pleasing expression and winning smile, and when she spoke I thought I had never heard such a musical voice.[2]

Her biographer tells of her timid nature and how she was nervous to speak to a crowd of men in her home country.[3]

Toward the end of her life, Mary wrote to a supporter:

I have always said that I have no idea how or why God has carried me over so many funny and hard places, and made these hordes of people submit to me, or why the Government should have given me the privilege of a Magistrate among them, except in answer to prayer made at home for me. It is all beyond my comprehension. The only way I can explain it is on the ground that I have been prayed for more than most. Pray on, dear one—the power lies that way.[4]

As she repeatedly ran through the jungle to prevent bloodshed or rescue an infant, she would pray. She said,

My one great consolation and rest . . . is in prayer. . . . I did not use [sic] to believe the story of Daniel in the lions dens [sic] . . . until I had to take some of these awful marches, and then I knew it was true, and that it was written for my comfort. Many a time I walked along praying, "O God of Daniel shut their mouths," and He did.[5]

Slessor did not become this woman of faith overnight. When she was a child, her alcoholic father wasted the family's money. After his death, responsibility for providing for the family fell to her, the oldest daughter. By age fourteen, Slessor was working ten hours per day in a textile factory. She often balanced a book on top of her loom to read whenever she could during the workday.

She read much about mission work in Africa. Then in 1874, David Livingstone's death inspired young Slessor to take the gospel to Africa.[6] After some training and arrangements for the care of her family, twenty-eight-year-old Slessor sailed for Nigeria on August 5, 1876.

For ten years, she served alongside veteran missionaries near the harbor, but the call of the unreached, inland tribes tugged at her heart. During this time, she wrote,

It is difficult to wait. . . . Christ never was in a hurry. . . . There was
no rushing forward, no anticipating, no fretting over what might
be. Every day's duties were done as every day brought them, and
the rest was left with God. "He that believeth shall not make haste"
(Isaiah 28:16).[7]

As Mary kept considering a move into the dangers of the
untamed north, her mother assured her, "You are my child, given
to me by God . . . and I have given you back to Him. When He
needs you and where He sends you, there I would have you be."[8]
Not long after this, God took her mother and younger sister
home to heaven. Mary wrote, "Heaven is now nearer to me than
Britain, and no one will be anxious about me if I go up-country."[9]
In 1888, with permission from her mission board, she ventured
into the realm of martyrs.

Over the next fifteen years, despite her enormous social influence on the region, Mary Slessor struggled with the lack of
spiritual results. Many days were consumed with caring for the
growing family of orphans she had rescued or beating back the
jungle around her hut. She wrote, "So, you see, life here, as at
home, is just a record of small duties which occupy the time, and
task the strength without much to show for it."[10] With so many
people needing help, she felt she had no choice. "I must put my
hands in wherever there is work to be done."[11] In all her practical
aid, she tried to share the life-giving message of the gospel, but
few showed any sign of a believing response.

"Yes, Ma," they would say, "that is right for you; but you and we are
different." But she never lost hope. "There is not much progress to
report," she was accustomed to say, "and yet very much to thank God
for, and to lead us to take courage. . . . It comes back to this, Christ
sent me to preach the Gospel, and He will look after results."[12]

In her letters, Slessor often repeated her burden to see genuine conversions among the people of Okoyong: "We have just kept on sowing the seed of the Word, believing that when God's time comes to gather them into the visible Church there will be some among us ready to participate in the privilege and honour."[13] Later she wrote, "I feel the smallness of the returns . . . but is the labour lost? A thousand times No!"[14]

In 1903, fifteen years after moving north, tears filled her eyes as coworkers led the first communion service in the region.[15] As the fledgling church grew, she encouraged the believers: "Okoyong now looks to you more than to me for proof of the power of the Gospel."[16]

Since she knew the results belong to God, Slessor often emphasized her reliance on prayer. She wrote, "Prayer can do anything; let us try its power."[17] In another letter, she affirmed, "My life is one long daily, hourly, record of answered prayer. . . . I can testify with a full and often wonder-stricken awe that I believe God answers prayer. I know God answers prayer."[18]

Toward the end of her life, as accolades began to pile up and more churches sprang up in the region, Slessor attributed the results to God, writing, "It isn't Mary Slessor doing anything, but Something outside of her altogether uses her as her small ability allows."[19] In another letter, she attested, "If I have done anything in my life it has been easy because the Master has gone before."[20] Responding to those who praised her work, Slessor asked rhetorically, "What would I do with starry crowns except to cast them at His feet?"[21] If God provides the results, then God should get the glory.

Today, few are pioneer missionaries venturing into trials by ordeal, slavery, and infanticide. However, every believer must look to God for fruit and lasting results from their labors. From the very first church planting efforts of the first century, God's power has grown His work. Paul wrote in 1 Corinthians 3:6, "I have planted, Apollos watered; but God gave the increase."

We often live like the increase depends on us. We pray as a duty rather than as a necessity. We fret when the methods we employ do not produce the results we expect. The results we seek can become our idols. Let us, like Slessor, seize the promises of God and say, "Christ sent me to preach the Gospel, and He will look after the results."

PERSONAL REFLECTION

- How do my prayers reflect my reliance on God for results?

- Am I willing to serve without seeing the spiritual fruit I desire?

- Have results become an idol in my life? How can I tell if I am laboring for results rather than faithfully serving for God's approval?

FURTHER READING   **1 Corinthians 3**

McLennan, Bruce. *Mary Slessor: A Life on the Altar for God.* Greanies House, UK: Christian Focus, 2014.

ABIDING
IN CHRIST

"Abiding, not striving nor struggling; looking off unto Him; trusting Him for present power; trusting Him to subdue all inward corruption; resting in the love of an almighty Saviour."

—JOHN MCCARTHY, MISSIONARY TO CHINA (1839–1911)

"Abide in me, and I in you. As the branch cannot bear fruit of itself, except it abide in the vine; no more can ye, except ye abide in me. I am the vine, ye are the branches: He that abideth in me, and I in him, the same bringeth forth much fruit: for without me ye can do nothing. . . . Herein is my Father glorified, that ye bear much fruit; so shall ye be my disciples."

—JOHN 15:4–8

The tiny sampan bumped over waves and weaved between junks on the Grand Canal in the Jiansu province of China. Hudson Taylor gripped his seat, overcome with exhaustion though the sun had only just risen on Saturday, September 4, 1869. Perhaps the quick trip to Yangzhou had been too soon after his illness. However, his coworker was even more ill than he had been, requiring Taylor's skill as a doctor. Perhaps the summer heat sucked away his energy. Perhaps the constant press of the crowds, the swarms of biting insects, and the putrid smells of the canal overwhelmed his senses. Though eager to get back to his headquarters in Zhenjiang, Taylor dreaded his return to the office. More meetings, correspondence, and decisions, backlogged by his two-week recovery from sickness, awaited him there. Alone for once on the sampan, Taylor's mind reverted to the despondent thoughts that had so frequently plagued him.

Taylor struggled to understand his feelings. He knew he should be rejoicing, not discouraged. God had blessed mightily in the four years since Taylor launched the China Inland Mission. The work grew, adding new missionaries, expanding to new cities, and multiplying converts and churches. Yet, the more the work succeeded, the heavier his burden felt. The more he labored, the more depleted he felt. More troubling, he endured a recurring spiritual emptiness and a growing frustration with his inability to overcome it. Masking his inner turmoil, Taylor soldiered on, drowning in the work.

Taylor disembarked near where the Grand Canal met the great Yangtze River. He wound his way through the bustling streets of Zhenjiang. Along the way, he encountered a few coworkers who returned with him to his headquarters. A crowd of missionaries had already gathered there for breakfast. When he could graciously get away, Hudson Taylor retired to his office where a tower of letters demanded his attention.

One letter changed everything.

The author of that letter was John McCarthy, an Irish friend and coworker serving in nearby Hangzhou. He, like Taylor, had been experiencing a consciousness of failure; a constant falling short of that which I felt should be aimed at; an unrest; a perpetual striving to find some way by which I might continuously enjoy that communion, that fellowship at times so real, but more often so visionary, so far off![1]

However, God had given McCarthy peace through the promises of John 15. In his letter, McCarthy followed his description of his spiritual struggle with the solution he found in God's Word:

Abiding, not striving nor struggling; looking off unto Him; trusting Him for present power; trusting Him to subdue all inward corruption; resting in the love of an almighty Saviour . . . this is not new, and yet 'tis new to me. . . . Christ . . . seems to me now the power, the only power for service; the only ground for unchanging joy.[2]

Taylor could not contain his excitement. He dashed up the rickety stairs to the sitting room and called his wife and coworkers to an impromptu meeting. Letter in hand, Taylor shared what McCarthy had taught him from God's Word.

Not long after that fateful morning, Taylor wrote to his sister. He praised God for his newfound freedom of soul and urged her to abide in Christ as she faced the daily rigors of raising her growing family in England. Taylor wrote,

But how to get faith strengthened? Not by striving after faith, but by resting on the Faithful One. . . . I have striven in vain to rest in Him. I'll strive no more. For has He not promised to abide with me—never to leave me, never to fail me? And, dearie, He never will! But this was not all He showed me, nor one half. As I thought of the Vine and the branches, what light the blessed Spirit poured direct [sic] into my soul! How great seemed my mistake in having wished to get the sap, the fulness out of Him. I saw not only that Jesus would never leave me, but that I was a member of His body, of His flesh and of His bones. . . . The sweetest part . . . is the rest which full identification with Christ brings . . . I am no better than before (may I not say, in

141

a sense, I do not wish to be, nor am I striving to be); but I am dead and buried with Christ—aye, and risen too and ascended; and now Christ lives in me, and "the life that I now live in the flesh, I live by the faith of the Son of God, Who loved me, and gave Himself for me." I now believe I am dead to sin. God reckons me so, and tells me to reckon myself so. He knows best. . . . I am as capable of sinning as ever, but Christ is realised as present as never before.[3]

The epiphany that McCarthy shared with Taylor has been called "Hudson Taylor's Spiritual Secret."[4] Yet, this truth is neither a secret nor something that Taylor had not read before. He wrote, "When my agony of soul was at its height, a sentence in a letter from dear McCarthy was used to remove the scales from my eyes, and the Spirit of God revealed the truth of our oneness with Jesus as I had never known it before."[5] Taylor had studied the theology of being "in Christ," but now he lived it, resting on Christ's strength to do the work and to carry the burden of responsibility.[6]

A month after reading McCarthy's letter, Taylor could testify,

As to work, mine was never so plentiful, so responsible, or so difficult; but the weight and strain are all gone. The last month or more has been perhaps, the happiest of my life; and I long to tell you a little of what the Lord has done for my soul. I do not know how far I may be able to make myself intelligible about it, for there is nothing new or strange or wonderful—and yet, all is new![7]

From that time on, abiding in Christ permeated Taylor's life, writings, and sermons.[8] In the China Inland Mission publication *China's Millions*, Taylor wrote in 1875, "The branch of the vine does not worry, and toil, and rush here to seek for sunshine, and there to find rain. No; it rests in union and communion with the vine; and at the right time, and in the right way, is the right fruit found on it. Let us so abide in the Lord Jesus."[9] Writing to his wife in September of 1878, during a time of financial trouble, he reminded her, "We must all get nearer to God; we must all abide in Christ."[10] Speaking to students in the Student Volunteer Movement in 1888, he chose the topic of abiding in Christ. Just months before his death in 1905, Taylor encouraged new missionaries that "[Christ] is near, nearer than we think. The Lord Jesus will never leave nor forsake us. Count on Him: enjoy Him: abide in Him."[11]

Few today have heard of John McCarthy, but his encouragement to Hudson Taylor to live the promise of abiding in Christ influenced both his leader and his entire mission. McCarthy served faithfully for forty years, opening Anhui, Yunnan, and Szechuan to the gospel. In 1884, God used McCarthy to preach a sermon in London that compelled the famous cricketer C. T. Studd to give up his career for missionary work in China.[12] In addition, McCarthy's two sons, Frank and William, followed in their father's footsteps as missionaries to China. John McCarthy's abiding life bore fruit in the lives of others.

Does my heart yearn to bear spiritual fruit? God promises that bearing fruit comes through abiding in Christ. Without abiding in Christ, I cannot bear fruit. He is the vine. I am a branch. The branch can only produce fruit by sucking its strength from the vine. Genuine, lasting spiritual fruit in my life and through me in others' lives only comes as I rely on Christ. This fruit, produced by God, brings glory to Him.

PERSONAL REFLECTION

- Where do I find the ability to live a holy life in service to God?

- Do I live like Christianity is a list of rules or a pile of responsibilities that I must shoulder on my own? Am I striving to serve God in my own strength?

- How can I let Christ live His life through me? (Galatians 2:20)

- Do I rest on my identity with Christ? Have I realized that I died with Christ, was buried with Christ, and rose with Christ? (Romans 6:1–13)

- Am I at this moment abiding in Christ?

FURTHER READING   **John 15:1–16**

Taylor, Dr. & Mrs. Howard. *Hudson Taylor and the China Inland Mission: The Growth of a Work of God.* Singapore: OMF International, 1918.

DAY 24

◀

PASSING
THE BATON

"There at the graveside I also picked up the baton he had held—the baton of forgiveness."[1]
—STEPHEN METCALF, MISSIONARY TO JAPAN (1927–2014)

"And I heard a voice from heaven saying unto me, Write, Blessed are the dead which die in the Lord from henceforth: Yea, saith the Spirit, that they may rest from their labours; and their works do follow them."
—REVELATION 14:13

The rough casket chafed seventeen-year-old Steve Metcalf's hands as he and his fellow prisoners bore Eric Liddell's body to its final resting place on February 24, 1945. The winter wind froze tears on the boy's cheeks, but his feet were warm. Liddell's running shoes, a gift to the boy just a few weeks before, protected Steve's feet. Those tattered shoes trudged through the mud to a small burial plot in a restricted corner of the Japanese internment camp in Shandong, China.

Since his incarceration over two years before, Liddell had adopted the young people imprisoned in the camp with him. Separated from his own three daughters by World War II, Liddell spent much of his spare time with the children of the camp, especially those separated from their families. One of these youths was Steve Metcalf, whose parents served as missionaries hundreds of miles away in the southwestern province of Yunnan. Liddell taught science in the camp's makeshift school and led the athletic program. Though Liddell was in his early forties, Metcalf and the other youths strove in vain to outrun the Olympic champion.[2]

Memories flooded Metcalf's mind as he set the casket down near a gaping hole in the ground. Resentment against his Japanese captors and the war that had robbed him of his mentor welled up in his heart. These emotions clashed with the words Liddell shared during the hours he spent discipling the youths. As he often did, Liddell had quoted from Christ's Sermon on the Mount:

> Matthew five includes the words, "Pray for those who persecute you." We spend time praying for the people we love, the people we like. But Jesus told us to pray for those we don't like. When you hate, you are self-centred. When you pray, you are God-centred. Praying changes your attitude. It is hard to hate those you pray for.[3]

Metcalf never forgot these words, nor did he forget Liddell's example.

As shovelfuls of dirt thudded against the casket, slowly hiding it from view, God began to change Metcalf's heart. He started praying a new prayer. He later wrote of that prayer, saying, "I told God that if I made it out of the camp alive, I would go to Japan as a missionary."[4]

Seven months later, God freed Metcalf from the internment camp. After a few years of work and Bible training, Metcalf left his postwar home in Australia to serve in Japan as a missionary. He would stay for nearly forty years, preaching the gospel to the nation that had imprisoned him as a youth. Metcalf would later write of Liddell's influence, "There at the graveside I also picked up the baton he had held—the baton of forgiveness."[5]

Liddell never knew that he inspired this teenager to be a missionary to Japan. He never dreamed of the Japanese souls saved or the churches planted as a result of his influence. Liddell's legacy was not in past Olympic glory but in the advance of God's work—even to a country where he himself never served as a missionary. He passed the baton forward in the only race with eternal rewards.

Revelation 14:12–13 speaks of the lasting impact and eternal reward of faithful servants of God:

> Here is the patience of the saints: here are they that keep the commandments of God, and the faith of Jesus. And I heard a voice from heaven saying unto me, Write, Blessed are the dead which die in the Lord from henceforth: Yea, saith the Spirit, that they may rest from their labours; and their works do follow them.

Like Liddell and Metcalf, believers in the final years before Christ's return will suffer, yet their work will not die with them. God promises that "their works do follow them." God will not forget to reward His faithful servants. He will also continue to use what they have done for Him on earth. Like Abel, Liddell "being dead yet speaketh" (Hebrews 11:4). Faithfulness has a ripple effect that the faithful one may never see during his earthly life.

We must be faithful even if the chances of making a difference seem small. World War II stripped Liddell of his family, his ministry, his health, and finally his life. Circumstances beyond Liddell's control seemingly erased years of labor. The discipling book he wrote appeared destined never to leave the internment compound and would not be published until 1985, forty years after his death. After nearly two decades ministering across the globe in the U.K. and China, Liddell's world shrunk to the confines of a Japanese internment camp. Instead of echoing the despair around him, Liddell shone as a beacon of hope by God's grace. Liddell seized the opportunities to serve those suffering with him, and God used his efforts well beyond the walls of their camp.

However, our influence on others can be for good or for evil. Over time, true character will come out as it did in the crucible of the Weihsien internment camp. In 1 Timothy 5:24–25, Paul warns that "some men's sins are open beforehand, going before to judgment; and some men they follow after. Likewise also the good works of some are manifest beforehand; and they that are otherwise cannot be hid." The Sermon on the Mount that Liddell loved to teach puts it this way: "Ye shall know them by their fruits" (Matthew 7:16). What fruits are blossoming from my life? When pressure is applied, what fragrance comes out? Am I producing something that should be reproduced in others?

God commands me to pass the baton. Second Timothy 2:2 states, "And the things that thou hast heard of me among many witnesses, the same commit thou to faithful men, who shall be able to teach others also." The relay of lived-out truth must continue beyond me.

You never know whom you are inspiring—for good or for ill. Treat each person as if you will see them again. Invest in each relationship so that a piece of you goes with them when the Lord takes you to the next stage in your journey. When your journey is done, you will have passed the baton.

PERSONAL REFLECTION

- What kind of baton am I passing to others? Am I passing on an example of forgiveness of bitterness? Of hope or despair? Of a gospel-saturated life or a self-centered life?

- How am I investing in others? Do I pay attention to those whom others ignore?

- What am I purposefully doing to make disciples of Jesus Christ?

- How are those I influence more Christlike because of my example and words?

FURTHER READING   2 Timothy 2

Clements, Ronald. *In Japan the Crickets Cry: How Could Steve Metcalf Forgive the Japanese?* Oxford: Monarch Books, 2010.

DAY 25

PRAYERS
AND PAINS

"Prayers and pains through faith in Christ Jesus,
will do any thing."

—JOHN ELIOT (1604–1690)

"But they that wait upon the LORD shall renew their strength;
they shall mount up with wings as eagles; they shall run, and
not be weary; and they shall walk, and not faint."

—ISAIAH 40:31

No one went. For twenty-six years, no one took the gospel to the Native Americans of New England. When the pilgrims first set foot on Plymouth Rock in 1620, one of their stated goals in fleeing to the New World was "an inward zeal and great hope of laying some foundation or making way for propagating the kingdom of Christ to the remote ends of the earth, though they should be but as stepping stones to others."[1] However, the pilgrims' struggle to survive in a climate so different from what they had expected discouraged any serious effort to reach the native population.

Nine years later, the vision continued. The settlers designed a seal for the Massachusetts Bay Colony bearing the image of a Native American calling out in the words of Acts 16:9, "Come over and help us." The accompanying charter stated that a major purpose of their colony was "to win and incite the natives of that country to the knowledge and obedience of the only true God and Saviour of mankind and the Christian faith." However, no one stepped up to spearhead an effort.

In 1646, forty-two-year-old John Eliot, an immigrant from England, initiated the first ongoing ministry among the Native American tribes. Soon after his arrival in America fifteen years before, Eliot had accepted the pastorate at the church in Roxbury, Massachusetts, a position he would hold for sixty years. In addition to this full-time job, Eliot began making contacts with the native peoples nearby, laying the groundwork for his itinerant preaching among them.

When obstacles barred the path of the gospel, Eliot knew where to turn. He wrote, "That when we would have any great things to be accomplished, the best policy is to work by an engine which the world sees nothing of."[2] That engine was prayer.

Thus relying on God, Eliot tackled the first challenge—learning a Native American language few other English settlers knew, the local Massachusett dialect. Despite no language tools and an unfaithful assistant, Eliot learned to preach the gospel in the native tongue. Facing apathy and sometimes outright opposition from his nomadic audience, he continued to labor.

In the ensuing years, the Lord strengthened Eliot to establish congregations of what were then known as "praying Indians." Working within the colonial framework of his time, Eliot helped these new Native American Christians to build their own settlements, including Natick and Nonantum (now known as Newton, MA). In his writings, Eliot listed the spiritual questions the locals asked and his answers to them. He also recorded many individual accounts of Native Americans sharing their salvation testimonies.

By 1661, Eliot had reduced the spoken Massachussett language to writing and translated the New Testament. Not long after, he published the entire Bible in Massachussett, the first Bible translated and printed in America. In addition, Eliot published a catechism and a grammar. Toward the end of his grammar, he wrote, "Prayers and pains through faith in Christ Jesus, will do any thing."[3]

By the late 1660s, Eliot oversaw fourteen settlements of believing Native Americans. Eleven hundred individuals made professions of faith.[4] Other devout Englishmen joined in the mission, including Thomas Mayhew and his sons in Martha's Vineyard and James Fitch in Connecticut. Using the grammar Eliot produced, literacy among the natives grew, and Eliot and like-minded preachers trained local men to reach their own people.[5]

Suddenly, in 1675, King Philip's War decimated the growing work. Native American King Philip (also called Metacomet) led his warriors against the European colonists, trapping the "praying Indians" squarely in the middle of the bloody conflict.[6] Despised by King Philip's alliance and distrusted by the colonists, many believing Native Americans fled their new towns, never to return. By 1684, only four official settlements of "praying Indians" remained.

Well into his eighties, his life drawing to a close, John Eliot prayed for the revival of the Native American work: "There is a cloud, a dark cloud, upon the work of the gospel, among the poor Indians. . . . The Lord revive and prosper that work, and grant that it may live when I am dead."[7] His prayers would be answered in the next generation by the likes of David Brainerd and Jonathan Edwards.

Meanwhile, Eliot waited on the Lord. God promises, "But they that wait upon the LORD shall renew their strength; they shall mount up with wings as eagles; they shall run, and not be weary; and they shall walk, and not faint" (Isaiah 40:31). Waiting on God does not mean inaction. If that were so, why would waiting on God result in renewed strength to fly, run, and walk without giving up? Waiting and working go together. Prayer and pain are often friends, not foes. As believers, we are to be "rejoicing in hope; patient in tribulation; continuing instant in prayer" (Romans 12:12). Do these words describe us today?

The work of God is never easy. Culture, prejudice, and narrow-mindedness all prey on faithful servants of God, sucking their energy and distracting them from the work. Matters far beyond a believer's control can seemingly wipe out years of faithful labor. In our limited perspective, we cry out, questioning whether the toil and tears are worth such meager visible results.

Wait on the Lord. Pray. Let the Lord renew your strength. Work. Suffer. Do not give up. You are not alone. Faithful believers have gone before you. Others, if the Lord tarries, will follow. The victory is ours. As Eliot wrote in the back of his grammar, "Prayers and pains through faith in Christ Jesus, will do any thing."

PERSONAL REFLECTION

- Is there some spiritual work that I know needs to be accomplished but no one is rising to the challenge?
- Am I praying for someone to step into that work?
- Have I considered that someone could be *me*?

FURTHER READING   **Isaiah 40**

THE UNBOUND GOSPEL

"The whole world is now my parish."

—GEORGE WHITEFIELD, PREACHER TO THE UNITED KINGDOM AND THE AMERICAN COLONIES (1714-1770)

"Be not afraid of their faces: for I am with thee to deliver thee, saith the LORD."

—JEREMIAH 1:8

No! No! Knock his brains out! Down with him! Kill him at once!" In England, a Christian nation in the eighteenth century, mobs of Roman Catholics, Anglicans, and local hooligans hurled rocks with their threats. They assaulted independent preachers and their followers. Why? Because these men and women believed in the necessity of regeneration. To be a true Christian, "ye must be born again" (John 3:3).

This revival of gospel truth began with George Whitefield, an ordained Anglican preacher and one of the early leaders of the Methodist movement. In 1735, Whitefield found new life in Christ by grace through faith alone. Not long after him, Whitefield's two friends, John and Charles Wesley, were also born again after witnessing the simple faith of the Moravians. However, the nominal Christians throughout England, including a majority of pastors and priests, had no spiritual life.

Whitefield began to preach regeneration and confront the problem of dead religion. He bemoaned the influence of unregenerate clergy: "The reason why congregations have been so dead is because they have dead men preaching to them. How can dead men beget living children?"[1] This message, unpopular with the clergy in his denomination, got Whitefield blacklisted. Church doors formerly open to his preaching ministry slammed shut.

Undaunted, Whitefield took his message to the streets and fields outside the official churches. He quoted Luke 14:23, "Go out into the highways and hedges, and compel them to come in, that my house may be filled." In his journal, he wrote,

> Let not the adversaries say I have thrust myself out. No, they have thrust me out. And since the self-righteous men of this generation count themselves unworthy, I go out into the highways and hedges, and compel harlots, publicans and sinners to come in, that my Master's house may be filled.[2]

Whitefield soon encouraged John and Charles Wesley to shake off the confines of the church building for the freedom of preaching outdoors. The idea shocked both the brothers and all of England. No one dared to preach outside of a church building without the official sanction of the church!

The Wesleys searched the Scriptures for guidance. Should they follow Whitefield's lead and preach in the open air in Bristol? "Four times they came upon a verse that spoke of suffering or death, and [John] Wesley believed that were he to go to Bristol he would die. Nevertheless he declared, 'I go,' and Charles stated, 'I desired to die with him.'"[3]

These were no idle fears.

John Wesley in his journal described one of many life-threatening situations he faced as a result of this decision:

> At the west end of the town, seeing a door half open, I would have gone in, but a gentleman in the shop would not suffer me, saying they would pull the house down to the ground. However, I stood at the door and asked, "Are you willing to hear me speak?" Many cried out, "No! No! Knock his brains out! Down with him! Kill him at once!"[4]

Charles Wesley wrote of a similar circumstance:

> I had just named my text at St. Ives (Isa. 40:1) when an army of rebels broke in on us. . . . They began in a most outrageous manner, threatening to murder the people. . . . They broke the sconces, dashed the windows in pieces, tore away the shutters, benches, poor-box, and all but the stone walls. I stood silently looking on, but mine eyes were unto the Lord. . . . They beat and dragged the women about, particularly one of great age, and trampled on them without mercy. The longer they stayed the more they raged. . . . The ruffians fell to quarreling among themselves, broke the Town-Clerk's (their Captain's) head, and drove one another out of the room.[5]

In his journal, Whitefield related how the captain of a ship visited him late one night:

> He suddenly rose up, uttering the most abusive language, calling me dog, rogue, villain, &c, and beat me most unmercifully with his gold-headed cane. But my hostess and her daughter hearing me cry murder, rushed into the room and seized him by the collar; however, he disengaged himself from them, and repeated his blows upon me.[6]

Had not nearby residents intervened, Whitefield may not have survived that night. On another occasion, he narrowly escaped stoning in Dublin.

Despite violent attacks both on their persons and their character, Whitefield and his associates continued preaching the gospel, stressing the necessity of regeneration. True Christianity is spiritual, not merely societal, because each sin-deadened heart must be changed by God. The unbound gospel extends its offer of new life from above to every person and every place. Writing aboard a ship on his way to America in 1739, Whitefield declared, "The whole world is now my parish. Wheresoever my Master calls me I am ready to go and preach the everlasting Gospel."[7]

In his short biography of Whitefield about a century later, J. C. Ryle reported that during Whitefield's thirty-four-year ministry he preached an astounding 18,000 times. Ryle gives a record of Whitefield's itinerant ministry: "Fourteen times did he visit Scotland. Seven times did he cross the Atlantic, backward and forward. Twice he went over to Ireland. As to England and Wales, he traversed every county in them."[8]

God used Whitefield to return the true gospel to two continents. His efforts brought genuine Christianity back to churches dead with nominal religion. He broke the conventional bounds of his day, preaching whenever and wherever God gave opportunity.

Today's society expects people to keep their religious opinions to themselves. Spirituality is extolled but confined to its own sphere. We are pressured to never let it spill over into our workplaces or casual acquaintances. "Respect other beliefs," they say. By *respect*, they mean we should treat each opinion as equally legitimate regardless of truth. "Stay in your lane and leave others in theirs. Do not upset society with your exclusive beliefs."

However, true spiritual life comes only through Christ. Therefore, all spirituality is not equal. "Ye must be born again" is still God's message to both nominal Christians and those raised in other religions.

As we share an exclusive gospel requiring spiritual birth, God encourages us like He encouraged Jeremiah: "Be not afraid of their faces: for I am with thee to deliver thee, saith the LORD" (Jeremiah 1:8). The New Testament likewise gives us hope, saying,

> Blessed are ye, when men shall revile you, and persecute you, and shall say all manner of evil against you falsely, for my sake. . . . Let your light so shine before men, that they may see your good works, and glorify your Father which is in heaven. (Matthew 5:11, 16)

Make the world your parish. Don't let illegitimate hindrances keep you from preaching the gospel. Share the new life God gave to you when you were born again.

PERSONAL REFLECTION

- How does fear affect my obedience to the Great Commission?
- What excuses am I making for not sharing the gospel?
- What gospel opportunities am I ignoring because societal pressure or others' expectations?
- Does my testimony extend beyond Sundays? How does it shine at church, home, and work?

FURTHER READING **Jeremiah 1**

Dallimore, Arnold A. *George Whitefield: God's Anointed Servant in the Great Revival of the Eighteenth Century.* Wheaton, IL: Crossway, 1990.

THE AWFUL IMPORTANCE OF ETERNAL THINGS

"[I have] the awful importance of eternal things impressed on my mind."

—HENRY MARTYN, MISSIONARY TO INDIA AND IRAN (1781–1812)

"Being born again, not of corruptible seed, but of incorruptible, by the word of God, which liveth and abideth for ever. For all flesh is as grass, and all the glory of man as the flower of grass. The grass withereth, and the flower thereof falleth away: But the word of the Lord endureth for ever. And this is the word which by the gospel is preached unto you."

—1 PETER 1:23–25

Y ou had better say God is God, and Muhammad is the prophet of God,'" said the Vizier of Teheran, Persia (modern-day Iran). Henry Martyn stood alone surrounded by Muslims in the Vizier's audience chamber. Every eye focused on the thirty-one-

year-old Englishman who had come to present his Persian translation of the Bible to the Shah.

"God is God," began Martyn. The tension in the room eased
for a moment. "And Jesus is the Son of God."

Angry shouts filled the chamber.

"God is neither born nor begets!"

"What will you say when your tongue is burnt out for this
blasphemy?"

They "rose up, as if they would have torn me in pieces," Martyn
wrote in his journal.[1] However, on that day, June 12, 1812, God
protected both the translator and the translation. The threats of
the Vizier's men gave way to sneers of contempt as they exited the
chamber, leaving Martyn alone holding his Persian Bible. Despite
Martyn's daring work, neither the Muslim leaders of Persia nor
their followers showed interest in turning to Christ.

Years before, while serving in India from 1806 to 1811, Martyn
struggled with similarly fruitless evangelistic attempts among the
Hindus. On January 4, 1808, he vented his frustration in his journal: "Truly, if ever I see a Hindu a real believer in Jesus, I shall see
something more nearly approaching the resurrection of a dead
body than anything I have yet seen."[2] Yet, he would also write
during this time, "Faith has been chiefly called into exercise, and
without a simple dependence on the Divine promises I should
still every day sink into fatal despondency."[3]

Employment as a chaplain by the East India Company provided Martyn with inroads to regions not accessible to the tra-
ditional missionary at that time.[4] As a chaplain, he ministered
to European expatriates and colonial soldiers stationed in the
remote posts of India and then Persia. His direct preaching style

shocked the nominal Christians and compelled them to consider their lost state. However, Martyn felt most burdened to introduce the gospel to the unreached local residents.

Eventually, Martyn concluded that, despite his willingness to conduct itinerant evangelism in India among the local population,

> little permanent good . . . can be done till some of the Scriptures can be put into their hands. On this account I wish to help forward this work as quick [sic] as possible, because a chapter will speak plainly in a thousand places at once, while I can speak, and not very plainly, but in one.[5]

Encouraged by Baptist missionaries William Carey and Joshua Marshman in Serampore, Martyn used his unusual gifting in languages to further the pioneer work of God in India and the Middle East. In 1807, Martyn wrote,

> They wish to engage me as a translator of the Scriptures into Hindustani and Persian, by the help of some learned natives; and if this plan is settled at Calcutta, I shall engage in it without hesitation, as conceiving it to be the most useful way in which I can be employed at present in the Church of God.[6]

Plagued by chronic illness, spurned by the love of his life, and hampered by unfaithful assistants, Henry Martyn pursued Bible translation as his life's work. From what he wrote in his journal, he seemed to know that his time was short:

> Seven years have passed away since I was first called of God [to salvation]. Before the conclusion of another seven years, how probable is it that these hands will have mouldered into dust! But be it so: my soul through grace hath received the assurance of eternal life, and I see the days of my pilgrimage shortening without a wish to add to their number.[7]

With the premonition of his early demise, Martyn prayed, "Let me burn out for God."[8] Working at a furious pace, he finished the Hindustani translation of the New Testament in 1810. Then, in 1811, he moved to Iran to perfect his Persian translation. At the beginning of 1812, the year of his death, he wrote,

> To all appearance the present year will be more perilous than any I have seen, but if I live to complete the Persian New Testament, my life after that will be of less importance. But whether life or death be mine, may Christ be magnified in me. If He has work for me to do, I cannot die.[9]

God answered his prayers. Martyn would indeed burn out for God but not before he completed his life's work.

By October, exhausted and burning with fever, Martyn decided to return to England for rest. His journey ended before he reached Istanbul, Turkey. Whether he finally died of his chronic illness or of the bubonic plague that ravaged the region at the time is unknown, but Martyn's work was done.

Every life is short. Whether we live to age thirty-one like Martyn, or age eighty-two like John Paton, our time on this earth will come to an end. What matters is not the number of years we lived but what we have invested in eternity. What are we doing that will last beyond our lives?

Only three things in this world are eternal: human souls (Matthew 25:46), a believer's relationship with God (John 17:3), and the Word of God (Isaiah 40:6–8). Martyn sought to reach the first, cultivated the second, and opened the third to whole people groups who had never heard. He lived a short life that had eternal results.

First Peter 1:23–25 links these three eternal things:

Being born again, not of corruptible seed, but of incorruptible, by the word of God, which liveth and abideth for ever. For all flesh is as grass, and all the glory of man as the flower of grass. The grass withereth, and the flower thereof falleth away: But the word of the Lord endureth for ever. And this is the word which by the gospel is preached unto you."

As the countdown for every human life ticks toward zero, the plight of each eternal soul deepens. Only the gospel message, found in the Word of God, can rescue frail-like-grass humans and provide the new birth necessary to begin an everlasting relationship with the Creator.

Not only is God's Word eternal, but the Bible also has a lasting effect. "So shall my word be that goeth forth out of my mouth: it shall not return unto me void, but it shall accomplish that which I please, and it shall prosper in the thing whereto I sent it" (Isaiah 55:11). As the apostle Paul wrote, "Faith cometh by hearing, and hearing by the Word of God" (Romans 10:17). With confidence in the promised efficacy of God's Word, Henry Martyn burnt out his short life for God, spending it to translate God's eternal Word into the common language of millions of people.

Several months before he died, Martyn met with two earnest Jews in Iran. Under pressure, these men had converted to Islam. They told Martyn of their spiritual struggles to find the truth. Later that day, Martyn wrote in his journal that, as he listened to them groping for light in the darkness, he had "the awful importance of eternal things impressed on my mind."[10]

The importance of eternal things permeated Martyn's journals and influenced his daily life. Today, we may question the risks Martyn took or the way he took care of his health, but we dare not question his values. He treasured the eternal over the temporal. We would do well to do the same.

PERSONAL REFLECTION

- What are my top five priorities in life? Which is first?

- How do my values reveal what is most important to me?

- Where do I spend my time, money, and other resources?

- To what do I give a higher place than the three eternal things?

FURTHER READING   **1 Peter 1**

Smith, George. *Henry Martyn: Saint and Scholar, First Modern Missionary to the Mohammedans.* London: The Religious Tract Society, 1892.

CHOOSING THE HEAVY END

"If ten men are carrying a log, nine of them on the little end and one at the heavy end, and you want to help, which end will you lift on?"

—WILLIAM BORDEN, MISSIONARY TO EGYPT (1887–1913)

"And Jesus answered and said, Verily I say unto you, There is no man that hath left house, or brethren, or sisters, or father, or mother, or wife, or children, or lands, for my sake, and the gospel's, But he shall receive an hundredfold now in this time, houses, and brethren, and sisters, and mothers, and children, and lands, with persecutions; and in the world to come eternal life."

—MARK 10:29–30

Most missionaries launch their ministries as unknowns and die as unknowns—but not William Borden. Born in 1887 to millionaires in Chicago, Borden enjoyed fame and fortune. Growing up as a prominent member of the Moody church under R. A. Torrey, Borden quickly rose to prominence in Christian circles. As a college student, he served as an influential delegate to the student volunteer movement.[1] By age twenty-two, while still a student, he joined the boards of the Moody Bible Institute and the China Inland Mission. As he studied at Yale University (1905–1909) and then Princeton Seminary (1909–1912), his name frequented the newspapers as Americans followed the career of this wealthy heir to the Borden family fortune.[2] Few missionaries have this pedigree or influence.

William Borden stunned the world when he turned his back on his fame and fortune to be a missionary to the Uyghur Muslims in northwestern China. A classmate from Princeton reflected the feelings of many when he said Borden was "throwing himself away as a missionary." Borden, remembering a trip around the world that he had taken during his high school years, replied, "You have not seen heathenism."[3] The plight of the lost gripped his heart, and the call of the Great Commission stirred him to action.

As Borden prepared to leave for the mission field, he accepted many invitations to speak across America. During these speeches he would often challenge his listeners: "If ten men are carrying a log, nine of them on the little end and one at the heavy end, and you want to help, which end will you lift on?"[4] Borden, despite his privileged background and the wide influence he had in America, determined to lift on the heavy end. He would spearhead an effort to go where the workers were few and the harvest was difficult. He sought to establish a beachhead of truth where the darkness was thickest and the enemy the strongest.

Borden's decision echoed the mindset of the church's first pioneer missionary, the apostle Paul: "Yea, so have I strived to preach the gospel, not where Christ was named, lest I should build upon another man's foundation" (Romans 15:20). While he could have remained at the thriving church at Antioch, Paul chose to answer God's call, going to Asia Minor, Greece, Rome, and even Spain.

Pioneer missions today is not what it was during Borden's day. In the last century, the gospel has penetrated deeply into regions that once had no witnesses for Christ. However, the light is not spread evenly across the globe.

Furthermore, where light has gone before, the darkness unceasingly endeavors to snuff it out. The Middle East was the birthplace of Christianity. Europe was once the hub of Christianity on the planet. Generations far from God now dominate these regions.

Where are you lifting the name of Christ? What is keeping you from lifting on the heavy end? C. T. Studd, who launched several missionary efforts in Asia and Africa in the late 1800s and early 1900s, wrote, "Some wish to live within the sound of Church or Chapel bell, [but] I want to run a Rescue Shop within a yard of hell."[5] Where do you wish to live and minister for Christ?

Despite his determination to lift on the heavy end, Borden never actually served among the Uyghur people. God had other plans for the young man with the shining testimony. On his way to China, Borden stopped in Cairo, Egypt, for a few months of training in ministry to Muslims under Dr. Samuel Zwemer. To the shock of the Christian world, cerebral meningitis struck down the twenty-five-year-old before he could even begin what he thought would be his life's work.

As word of his death circled the world, God used the testimony of Borden's dedication to spur a wave of new missionaries to go and lift on the heavy end. A Princeton classmate wrote of Borden's passion and legacy: "No one would have known from

Borden's life and talk that he was a millionaire . . . but no one could have helped knowing that he was a Christian and alive for missions."[6] The death of this widely known Christian served to launch scores of unknown Christians to take the message of Christ to forgotten people groups like the Uyghurs.

After Borden's death, a story began circulating about a quote he scrawled in his personal Bible—"No reserves, no retreats, no regrets." According to these accounts, William wrote "no reserves" as a sixteen-year-old during his trip around the world. Seeing the needs of the millions without Christ, the young man decided to give his all as a missionary. Later, when he graduated from Princeton and turned down lucrative business opportunities, William added "no retreats" in the margin of his Bible. Finally, as he lay dying of meningitis in Egypt, he penned "no regrets." The Bible with these inscriptions has never been found. Possibly, the story originated from a line by Mrs. Howard Taylor in his 1926 biography: "No reserve, no retreat, no regrets had any place in Borden's consecration to God."[7] Whether genuine or apocryphal, the quote captures the essence of Borden's life and has motivated many to this day to go and lift on the heavy end.

PERSONAL REFLECTION

- What heavy end am I lifting? Which hard jobs have I avoided?

- Do I volunteer only when my comfort zone will not be affected?

- Could I go and labor in obscurity in some distant land? What about work among Muslims? How about among the poor?

- What relationships or possessions have priority over the cause of Christ in my life?

- Am I willing to choose the hard path even if the easy path is rolled out before me?

FURTHER READING   **Philippians 3**

Taylor, Mrs. Howard. *Borden of Yale '09: The Life that Counts.* Philadelphia: China Inland Mission, 1957.

DAY 29

NO SACRIFICE

"I never made a sacrifice."

—DAVID LIVINGSTONE, MISSIONARY TO AFRICA (1813–1873)

"For whosoever will save his life shall lose it;
but whosoever shall lose his life for my sake and the gospel's,
the same shall save it."

—MARK 8:35

With terrifying speed, the lion bore down on David Livingstone. Bullets whizzed through the air and sunk into the beast to no avail. The lion's mighty jaws clamped down on the thirty-one-year-old missionary's shoulder. Livingstone could hear the sickening crunch of his bones as the lion's weight pushed him to the dust. With the lion's paw pressing his head to the ground, Livingstone wondered "what part of me he would eat first."

"Yah, yah," his African assistant Mebalwe screamed, running toward the beast. With a final jolt, the lion leapt off the injured man. With his vision blurred by pain and a swirling cloud of dust, Livingstone watched the lion pounce on Mebalwe, tearing into his thigh. More shots rang out. The lion's invincibility expired, and the great beast fell to the ground.[1]

Both Livingstone and Mebalwe survived the attack, but for the next thirty years, Livingstone's left arm was never the same. Friends reported that he could no longer lift his arm above his shoulder without great pain. After such a frightening experience and injury, many would have left Africa—but not Livingstone. He had much more to lose for the cause of Christ in the wilds of Africa.

Livingstone's path of sacrifice took a circuitous route that revealed the guiding hand of providence. Before ever considering going to Africa, Livingstone read of the millions without the gospel in China. Burdened to reach them, he studied medicine to prepare for a work there. However, in 1839, the First Opium War closed that door.

As Livingstone wondered where he could serve and use his medical training, the Lord brought veteran missionary Robert Moffat into his life. Moffat encouraged the young man to join him in South Africa and "advance to unoccupied ground, specifying the vast plain to the north, where I had sometimes seen, in the morning sun, the smoke of a thousand villages, where no missionary had ever been."[2] No sooner had Livingstone caught that vision than a liver ailment nearly took his life. This brush with death in the friendly confines of home would prepare him to face disease in the uncharted regions of Africa.

Livingstone's goal, despite personally acknowledging he was not a great preacher, was to bring the gospel to Africa. In 1850, Livingstone wrote to his father, "I am a missionary, heart and soul. God had an only Son, and He was a missionary and a physician. A poor, poor imitation of Him I am, or wish to be. In this service I hope to live, in it I wish to die."[3]

Upon his arrival in Africa in 1841, Livingstone encountered setback after setback. He expected dangers of wild animals and diseases, but the greatest obstacles proved to be fellow Europeans and the slave trade. Furthermore, his preaching produced little fruit, and a prominent chief who professed faith in Christ soon fell into sin.

During this trying time, God opened opportunities for Livingstone to venture short distances away from his mission station. On these trips of discovery, the young missionary found his niche in the Lord's work. Years before, Livingstone had written, almost prophetically, to a friend, "Whatever way my life may be spent so as but to promote the glory of our gracious God, I feel anxious to do it. . . . My life, may be spent as profitably as a pioneer as in any other way."[4]

By 1852, Livingstone had abandoned settled ministry, taking long treks into territories unmapped by any European. As he contacted new peoples and charted new paths across south and central Africa, he paved the way for more effective preachers and evangelists to follow. In addition, his determined fight against slavery in Africa—whether the master be European, Arab, or African—helped to divorce Christian missions from the wicked slave trade in the minds of the African people of the regions he traveled. Through trials and hardships, God's hand guided Livingstone into his life's work which would open inland Africa to the gospel message.

In December of 1857, Livingstone, now age forty-four and at home for his first furlough, addressed an assembly at Cambridge University:

> For my own part, I have never ceased to rejoice that God has appointed me to such an office. People talk of the sacrifice I have made in spending so much of my life in Africa. Can that be called a sacrifice which is simply paid back as a small part of a great debt

owing to our God, which we can never repay? Is that a sacrifice which brings its own blest reward in healthful activity, the consciousness of doing good, peace of mind, and a bright hope of a glorious destiny hereafter? Away with the word in such a view, and with such a thought! It is emphatically no sacrifice. Say rather it is a privilege. Anxiety, sickness, suffering, or danger, now and then, with a foregoing of the common conveniences and charities of this life, may make us pause, and cause the spirit to waver, and the soul to sink; but let this only be for a moment. All these are nothing when compared with the glory which shall hereafter be revealed in and for us. I never made a sacrifice.[5]

How could Livingstone say, "I never made a sacrifice"? Did he really make no sacrifice? Did Hudson Taylor, who made the same claim, make no sacrifice?[6] In one sense, their lives were full of sacrifice: sacrificed time, talents, health, and families. However, these men compared their losses not to what they could have had, but to the debt they owed Christ. They compared what they gave up to the glory awaiting them in the future (Romans 8:18). Whatever losses they suffered in the service to Christ, they counted as gain (Philippians 3:7–14).

Livingstone lived the promise of Mark 8:34–35, where Jesus declared, "Whosoever will come after me, let him deny himself, and take up his cross, and follow me. For whosoever will save his life shall lose it; but whosoever shall lose his life for my sake and the gospel's, the same shall save it." In the economy of Christ, personal loss for the Savior and the gospel is ultimately no sacrifice.

When we stand before the Judgment Seat of Christ, whatever we gave up in this life for the cause of Christ will seem insignificant (2 Corinthians 5:10). God promises to reward those who faithfully serve and sacrifice for Him (1 Corinthians 3:12–14). We should not fear loss. We should not dread sacrifice.

PERSONAL REFLECTION

- What should I sacrifice to more fully live for Christ? Does this worry me?

- How would viewing sacrifice in the Christian life as "I get to do this" rather than "I have to do this" change my attitude?

- Do I compare my losses with what I feel I deserve now or with what Christ has promised in His Word regarding the future?

FURTHER READING   **Mark 8:34–38**

BE FORGOTTEN

"Be content to suffer, die and be forgotten."

—NICHOLAS LUDWIG VON ZINZENDORF (1700–1760)

*"Humble yourselves in the sight of the Lord,
and he shall lift you up."*

—JAMES 4:10

Zinzendorf? A name like that is memorable. Count Nicholas Ludwig von Zinzendorf? His position, wealth, and prominence in society demands attention—at least in Germany of the eighteenth century. However, few Christians today have heard of him or recognize his influence on Christianity.

Raised by his devout grandmother, Zinzendorf trusted Christ for salvation as a young child, and his spiritual life blossomed under godly influences. Philipp Spener, the Father of Pietism, was a family friend. One of his teachers was August Francke, who led the Pietist movement after Spener's death.[1] During his schooling, Zinzendorf showed great spiritual sensitivity and a desire to please God. As a teenager, he began gathering small communities of believers together at his school to promote evangelism and mutual godliness.

In 1719 while traveling in Dusseldorf, eighteen-year-old Zinzendorf viewed a painting called *Ecce Homo* ("Behold the Man"), depicting Christ's suffering. Beneath the picture, he read the inscription: "All this I did for thee. What hast thou done for me?"[2] One hundred thirty-nine years later, the same painting and inscription in Dusseldorf would inspire hymn-writer Frances Havergal to write:

> I gave My Life for thee,
> My precious blood I shed
> That thou might'st ransomed be,
> And quickened from the dead.
> I gave My life for thee:
> What hast thou given for Me?[3]

Moved by the visualization of Christ's suffering and the pointedness of the question below it, Zinzendorf's passion for Christ increased. He sought out ways to use his wealth and social standing to further the gospel of Jesus Christ. He would write, "I have but one passion—it is He, it is He alone. The world is the field and the field is the world; and henceforth that country shall be my home where I can be most used in winning souls for Christ."[4] In the early eighteenth century, few shared Zinzendorf's burning passion for Christ and the Great Commission.

By 1722, Christian David, a young carpenter, introduced Zinzendorf to a group of persecuted Christians from his hometown in Moravia (a region in the modern-day Czech Republic). These believers needed a place of refuge from the persecution of the Roman Catholic Church. Zinzendorf invited these spiritual descendants of the historic reformer John Huss to move to his estate, where they established a village they called *Herrnhut*.

In the following years, the stream of refugees from Moravia and neighboring Bohemia continued and increased. Zinzendorf became their patron and leader. By 1731, Zinzendorf had resigned his official government positions to spend his time among the Moravians. Together, they would launch a missions movement across four continents. Zinzendorf himself would travel through Europe, the American colonies, and the West Indies to further their gospel work.[5]

In a letter to Moravian missionaries abroad, dated May 27, 1742, Zinzendorf wrote,

> Our method of proclaiming salvation is this: to point out to every heart the loving Lamb, who died for us, and although He was the Son of God, offered Himself for our sins . . . by the preaching of His blood, and of His love unto death, even the death of the cross, never, either in discourse or in argument, to digress even for a quarter of an hour from the loving Lamb: to name no virtue except in Him, and from Him and on His account, to preach no commandment except faith in Him; no other justification but that He atoned for us; no other sanctification but the privilege to sin no more; no other happiness but to be near Him, to think of Him and do His pleasure; no other self denial but to be deprived of Him and His blessings; no other calamity but to displease Him; no other life but in Him.[6]

Like the apostle Paul in 1 Corinthians 2:2, Zinzendorf and the Moravians "determined not to know any thing . . . save Jesus Christ, and him crucified."

Zinzendorf's impassioned emphasis on the gospel saturated not only his preaching but also his hymn-writing. During his lifetime, he penned nearly 2,000 hymns. One hymn, translated from German by John Wesley, is still sung in English-speaking churches today:

Jesus, Thy blood and righteousness
My beauty are, my glorious dress;
Midst flaming worlds, in these arrayed,
With joy shall I lift up my head.

Bold shall I stand in that great Day,
For who aught to my charge shall lay?
Fully absolved through these I am
From sin and fear, from guilt and shame.

Lord, I believe Thy precious blood,
Which at the mercy-seat of God
Forever doth for sinners plead,
For me—e'en for my soul—was shed.

Lord, I believe were sinners more
Than sands upon the ocean shore,
Thou hast for all a ransom paid,
For all a full atonement made.

When from the dust of death I rise
To claim my mansion in the skies,
E'en then, this shall be all my plea:
Jesus hath lived and died for me.

This first generation of Moravians, like their Savior before them, humbled themselves to reach the world with the gospel. Beginning in 1732, the Moravians sent missionaries to Greenland, across the Americas, and all the way to South Africa. The missionary spirit among them was so great that one out of every twelve Moravians left Germany as a foreign missionary.[7] Some Moravians serving in the Caribbean went so far as to become slaves in order to reach the slaves.

In a speech at Herrnhut, on January 19, 1758, Zinzendorf exhorted a group of departing missionaries:

> You must never try to lord over the heathen, but rather humble yourself among them, and earn their esteem through the power of the Spirit. . . . Like the cab-horses in London, he [the missionary] must wear blinkers and be blind to every danger and to every snare and conceit. He must be content to suffer, to die and be forgotten.[8]

Few today remember Zinzendorf and the Moravian missionary movement. They preached the gospel, died, and were forgotten. Names like John Wesley and William Carey glow in the limelight of history, but without Zinzendorf and the Moravians, there may never have been a Wesley or Carey. Through the testimony of poor Moravian missionaries on a ship to Georgia, Wesley came to a saving knowledge of Christ. Through the example of Zinzendorf and the Moravians, Carey caught a vision for world missions.

The history of Christianity is populated with millions of the forgotten faithful. Most are never immortalized. From the catacombs of Rome in the first century to the tent-making witnesses in the Middle East today, God's people suffer, die, and are forgotten by this world.

God gives the forgotten this promise in James 4:10: "Humble yourselves in the sight of the Lord, and he shall lift you up." When will we be lifted up? Maybe not in this life, but God will never forget us. In Hebrews 6:10, God promises, "For God is not unrighteous to forget your work and labour of love, which ye have shewed toward his name." Our ultimate exaltation still awaits us in Christ's kingdom.

PERSONAL REFLECTION

- If no one notices, values, or remembers my service to Christ, what will keep me from giving up?

- Is Christ alone my passion? What other passions compete with my passion for Him?

- Have I surrendered to preach the gospel, die, and be forgotten?

FURTHER READING   **2 Corinthians 5**

ALL THINGS NEW

"Oh! when shall time give place to eternity?
When shall appear that new heaven and new earth
wherein dwelleth righteousness?"

—THE LAST JOURNAL ENTRY OF HENRY MARTYN,
MISSIONARY TO INDIA AND IRAN (1781–1812)

"Behold, I make all things new."
—REVELATION 21:5

Henry Martyn dashed out of the former Indian pagoda that temporarily served as his home. The fire of a nearby funeral pyre danced in the sky. "I ran out," he wrote in his journal afterward, "but the unfortunate woman had committed herself to the flames before I arrived." Seared on his memory were the images of the charred remains of the immolated widow. "I do not know when I was so shocked; my soul revolted at everything in this world."[1]

Corruption and perversion mar God's once-perfect creation. The sin of mankind seems to defy all protestations of hope. The blood spilled on every continent testifies to the darkness of depravity. The cries of children sold by their parents into temple prostitution rang out to God from India. In Papua, Indonesia, loving parents threw toddlers to their deaths in powerful waterfalls, and villagers hungered for the flesh of their neighbors across the gorges. In China, foot-bound women toddled around while marauding bands of savage men rampaged across the countryside, beheading innocent peasants. In the Middle East, genocide and conquest nearly erased Christianity from the lands of its inception. In Africa, parents slaughtered twin babies, sold each other into slavery, and even raised some slaves for food. In Europe, hoards of Germanic tribes raped and pillaged broad swathes of the continent. Later, in more "civilized" times, colonial powers like Portugal, Great Britain, and France bought and sold slaves like livestock, and their colonies continued these horrors. In South America, ancient civilizations practiced human sacrifice, even of children. In North America, violent men scalped and murdered lonely settlers which led to atrocities like the Trail of Tears. No region of the earth has escaped the depravity of the human race.

The ruins of great civilizations lay buried across every continent, exposing the lie of the inevitable enlightenment of mankind over time. There is no upward path of progress. Primitive peoples are often remnants of once-glorious societies. The noble savage has never existed.

In the modern era, more sophisticated atrocities continue to occur. From the Holocaust to abortion, men and women justify their evil deeds. The depth of darkness in this world is unfathomable. As Jesus declared, "Men loved darkness rather than light, because their deeds were evil" (John 3:19). Paul further explained, "When they [sinners] knew God, they glorified him not as God, neither were thankful; but became vain in their imaginations, and their foolish heart was darkened" (Romans 1:21).

But light has come into this world (John 3:19). Though no man seeks after God, God seeks after man (Romans 3:10–11;

Luke 19:10). As His light awakens their consciences, individuals call for help out of the darkness (Acts 10:2, 21–22; 16:30).

As the light just began reaching the jungles of Nigeria, a chief begged for more missionaries: "Tell them that our need is great, and that we are in darkness and waiting for the light."[2] Mary Slessor said, "God is always in the world. . . . The sunshine will break out and light will triumph."[3] Edward Judson spoke of gospel light, as well: "We looked back on the centuries of darkness that are past. We looked forward, and Christian hope would fain brighten the prospect. Perhaps we stand on the dividing line of the empires of darkness and light."[4] No doubt, God's people have stood on that line through the centuries. Having been drawn by God into the light, we, the servants of God, beckon to those behind us to cross with us from darkness into light.

After his conversion to Christ, Sar, a former spirit priest and cannibal of Papua, Indonesia, testified of God's power to change lives:

> Now these men [both local believers and missionaries] are laying down their lives so that others need not die as they did. I cannot deny any longer: this new way is better. Come, let us believe on Jesus Christ. I see now that He can change our whole world. As Stan Dale kept telling us through the years, Christ can make all things new.[5]

This is Christ's promise and our hope: "I make all things new." The world-that-now-is stinks of rottenness to its core. Its stench fills our nostrils and nauseates us. The whole creation groans. Yet, change has already begun.

We, who have trusted Christ for salvation, have been born again. We have new life. "If any man be in Christ, he is a new creature: old things are passed away; behold, all things are become new" (2 Corinthians 5:17). Out of everything God made, we are the first to become new: "Of his own will begat he us with the word of truth, that we should be a kind of firstfruits of his creatures" (James 1:18). The spiritual transformation wrought within us breathes hope into a world pining incoherently for resurrection.

"I make all things new." This promise steels the hearts of believers to carry on, though disgusted by their own lapses into sin. This promise sustains God's people as they struggle against both overt opposition and immovable apathy. The deterioration surrounding us will not always be. The ages-long battle is not eternal. Victory is sure. Transformation is guaranteed.

Henry Martyn, thinking about these promises on December 31, 1811, wrote in his journal:

> The accounts of the desolations of war during the last year, which I have been reading in some Indian newspapers, make the world appear more gloomy than ever. How many souls hurried into eternity unprepared! How many thousands of widows and orphans left to mourn! But admire, my soul, the matchless power of God, that out of this ruin He has prepared for Himself an inheritance. At last the scene shall change, and I shall find myself in a world where all is love.[6]

Just hours before he entered that world of love, Martyn wrote his final journal entry:

> Oh! when shall time give place to eternity? When shall appear that new heaven and new earth wherein dwelleth righteousness? There, there shall in no wise enter in any thing that defileth: none of that wickedness which has made men worse than wild beasts, none of those corruptions which add still more to the miseries of mortality, shall be seen or heard of any more.[7]

Is this my hope? Do I yearn for a new world? Do I "according to his promise, look for new heavens and a new earth, wherein dwelleth righteousness" (2 Peter 3:13)? When I hear Christ's promise, "Surely I come quickly," does my heart cry, "Even so, come, Lord Jesus" (Revelation 22:20)? Come, and finish what you have begun (Philippians 1:6). Come, and make all things new.

PERSONAL REFLECTION

- When the darkness of this world depresses me, do I turn to God's promises of the new heaven and new earth?

- How does my life shine forth the reality of the change that is to come to all of creation when God makes all things new?

- How can I encourage others in dark times with the promises of God?

- How can I better live God's promises?

FURTHER READING   **Romans 8:18–39**

CONCLUSION

JOURNEY DEBRIEF

"Wherefore seeing we also are compassed about with so great a cloud of witnesses, let us lay aside every weight, and the sin which doth so easily beset us, and let us run with patience the race that is set before us, Looking unto Jesus the author and finisher of our faith; who for the joy that was set before him endured the cross, despising the shame, and is set down at the right hand of the throne of God."

—HEBREWS 12:1-2

Having glimpsed the testimonies of these who lived the promises of God, let us, as they did, look unto Jesus. Let us rest, as they did, on His promises. Let us focus on the eternal joy set before us and faithfully serve and endure. Let us abandon sin and every affection that would hinder His work in us and through us. Let us live lives worthy of biographies though they never be written.

I pray that after you finish this final chapter you will move on to reading the Christian biographies that inspired this devotional. A wealth of spiritual enrichment awaits you. This devotional has barely scratched the surface of the treasures you will find in reading about those in whom and through whom God has worked.

Do not stop with this short devotional. You are in the shallow end of the pool. Go to the deep end.

In the following pages, I have included a missionary biography checklist, arranged somewhat subjectively as either "must-read biographies" or "worth-reading biographies." The categorization of these books is in no way a critique of the lives of these dear men and women of God. Hopefully, the arrangement will provide a launching point for your future reading.

The must-read biographies are well-written and spiritually deep. They will challenge your walk with God. Through the many direct quotations and first-hand accounts in these biographies, you will gain a clearer picture of who they were.

The worth-reading biographies may be more difficult to get through. Some are more scholarly. Others are older works written in somewhat archaic styles. However, each of the biographies in this section will reward your digging for the spiritual nuggets buried within.

I expect that not everyone will agree with my classifications of these biographies. If you read enough of these books to form an opposing opinion, then these lists have done their work. Within the two categories, the biographies are listed alphabetically by author, so you can read the books in any order according to your own preference.

May the Lord bless all who read of these faithful servants of the Lord. Their lives are significant, not because they are worthy, but because their Lord is worthy. Their examples are deserving of emulation, not because they are better than we are, but because they lived out the promises of God's Word. We follow them as they followed Christ (1 Corinthians 11:1). As we see Christ in them, let us look to Christ.

THE ESSENTIAL MISSIONARY BIOGRAPHY CHECKLIST

MUST-READ BIOGRAPHIES

☐ *To the Golden Shore: The Life of Adoniram Judson* by Courtney Anderson

☐ *David Brainerd: A Flame for God* by Vance Christie

☐ *The Shadow of the Almighty: The Life and Testament of Jim Elliot* by Elisabeth Elliot

☐ *Through Gates of Splendor* by Elisabeth Elliot

☐ *By Searching: My Journey Through Doubt Into Faith* by Isobel Kuhn

☐ *The Autobiography of George Müller* by George Müller

☐ *The Story of John G. Paton: Thirty Years Among South Sea Cannibals* by John Paton

☐ *Lords of the Earth: An Incredible but True Story from the Stone-Age Hell of Papua's Jungle* by Don Richardson

☐ *Evidence Not Seen: A Woman's Miraculous Faith in the Jungles of World War II* by Darlene Deibler Rose

☐ *Behind the Ranges: Fraser of Lisuland* by Mrs. Howard Taylor

☐ *Hudson Taylor in Early Years: The Growth of a Soul* by Dr. and Mrs. Howard Taylor

☐ *Hudson Taylor and the China Inland Mission: The Growth of a Work of God* by Dr. and Mrs. Howard Taylor

☐ *The Triumph of John and Betty Stam* by Mrs. Howard Taylor

WORTH-READING BIOGRAPHIES

☐ *Robert Morrison: A Master-Builder* by Marshall Broomhall

☐ *William Carey* by S. Pearce Carey

☐ *Things as They Are: Mission Work in Southern India* by Amy Carmichael

☐ *John and Betty Stam: Missionary Martyrs* by Vance Christie

☐ *In Japan the Crickets Cry: How Could Steve Metcalf Forgive the Japanese?* by Ronald Clements

☐ *William Tyndale: A Biography* by David Daniell

☐ *George Whitefield: God's Anointed Servant in the Great Revival of the Eighteenth Century* by Arnold Dallimore

☐ *The Life and Diary of David Brainerd* by Jonathan Edwards

☐ *The Savage, My Kinsman* by Elisabeth Elliot

☐ *For the Glory: The Untold and Inspiring Story of Eric Liddell, Hero of Chariots of Fire* by Duncan Hamilton

☐ *Patrick of Ireland: His Life and Impact* by Michael Haykin

☐ *Mary Slessor: A Life on the Altar for God* by Bruce McLennan

☐ *Henry Martyn: Saint and Scholar, First Modern Missionary to the Mohammedans* by George Smith

☐ *George Müller: Delighted in God!* by Roger Steer

☐ *Lives of the Three Mrs. Judsons: Mrs. Ann H. Judson, Mrs. Sarah B. Judson, Mrs. Emily C. Judson, Missionaries to Burmah* by Arabella Stuart

☐ *Borden of Yale '09: The Life that Counts* by Mrs. Howard Taylor

NOTES

PREFACE — JOURNEY BRIEFING

1. A. W. Tozer, *Let My People Go: The Life of Robert A. Jaffray* (Camp Spring, PA: WingSpread Publishers, 2010), 5.
2. Jonathan Edwards, *The Life and Diary of David Brainerd with Notes and Reflections* (Peabody, MA: Hendrickson, 2006), preface.
3. Elisabeth Elliot, *A Chance to Die: The Life and Legacy of Amy Carmichael* (Old Tappan, NJ: Fleming H. Revell Company, 1987), 15.
4. Elisabeth Elliot, *The Shadow of the Almighty: The Life and Testament of Jim Elliot* (San Francisco: Harper Collins, 1958), 14.
5. J. C. Ryle, *A Sketch of the Life and Labors of George Whitefield* (New York: Anson D. F. Randolf, 1854), 7.

INTRODUCTION — THE STARTING POINT

1. Edward Judson, *The Life of Adoniram Judson* (New York : A. D. F. Randolph & Company, 1883), 12.

DAY 1 — J. HUDSON TAYLOR

1. Dr. & Mrs. Howard Taylor, *Hudson Taylor and the China Inland Mission: The Growth of a Work of God* (Singapore: OMF International, 1918), 31.
2. Ibid., 166.
3. Ibid., 252–253.
4. Ibid., 279.

DAY 2 — DARLENE DEIBLER ROSE

1. Darlene Deibler Rose, *Evidence Not Seen: A Woman's Miraculous Faith in the Jungles of World War II* (San Francisco: Harper & Row, 1988), 130.
2. Ibid., 45.
3. Ibid., 109.
4. Ibid., 141.
5. Ibid., 156.
6. Ibid., 156–157.
7. Personal Testimony of Darlene Deibler Rose, accessed on March 17, 2020. www.youtube.com/watch?v=T-BgTnkDJr4

DAY 3 — ADONIRAM JUDSON

1. Courtney Anderson, *To the Golden Shore: The Life of Adoniram Judson* (Valley Forge, PA: Judson Press, 1987), 322.
2. Edward Judson, *Adoniram Judson: A Biography* (Philadelphia: American Baptist Publication Society, 1883), 94.
3. Anderson, 403.

DAY 4 — JOHN PATON

1. John Gibson Paton, *The Story of John G. Paton: Thirty Years Among South Sea Cannibals* (New York: A. L. Burt Company, 1892), 108.
2. Ibid., 53.
3. Ibid., 108. Paton quoted Matthew 28:20; Philippians 4:13; and Hebrews 11:27.
4. Ibid., 123.
5. Ibid., 175.
6. Ibid., 181.

DAY 5 — JOHN STAM

1. Mrs. Howard Taylor, *The Triumph of John and Betty Stam* (Philadelphia: China Inland Mission, 1935), 104.
2. Ibid., 102–104.
3. Ibid., 54–55.
4. Ibid., 33.
5. Kathleen White, *John and Betty Stam: The Story of the Young American Missionaries Who Gave Their Lives for Christ and China* (Minneapolis: Bethany House Publishers, 1990), 118.
6. Taylor, *The Triumph of John and Betty Stam*, 105–106.
7. Ibid., 109.
8. Ibid., 109–110. Stam quoted Job 1:21.

DAY 6 — GEORGE LIELE

1. E. A. Holmes, "George Liele; Negro Slavery's Prophet of Deliverance," *Baptist Quarterly* (London: Baptist Historical Society, 1964): 346.
2. Ibid., 340.
3. At that time, a free person of any ethnicity could voluntarily indenture himself to a wealthy person, agreeing to act as their servant for a specified period of time to pay their travel expenses to another country or colony. Some, like author Doreen Morrison, claim Liele's indenture not only covered the passage but also repaid borrowed money used to buy the freedom of his wife and family. Doreen Morrison, *Slavery's Heroes: George Liele and the Ethiopian Baptists of Jamaica 1783–1865* (Jamaica: Liele Books, 2015), 29–33.
4. Terriel Byrd, "George Liele: Former Slave and First American Baptist Missionary," in *A Legacy of Preaching*, volume 2 (Grand Rapids, MI: Zondervan, 2018), 148–149.
5. Holmes, 341.
6. Ibid., 346.
7. Ibid., 351.

DAY 7 — JAMES O. FRASER

1. Mrs. Howard Taylor, *Behind the Ranges: Fraser of Lisuland* (London: Lutterworth Press and the China Inland Mission, 1944), 85.
2. Ibid., 47.
3. Ibid., 162.
4. Ibid., 125.
5. Ibid., 172–173.
6. Ibid., 129.
7. Ibid., 149.
8. Ibid., 228.
9. Ibid., 233.
10. Isobel Kuhn, *By Searching: My Journey Through Doubt Into Faith* (Chicago: Moody Press, 1959), 66.

DAY 8 — ISOBEL KUHN

1. Isobel Kuhn, *By Searching*, 47.
2. Frank H. Sweet, "A Noble Life," in *The Independent*, vol. LV (New York, 1903), 143.
3. Lois Hoadley Dick, *Isobel Kuhn: The Canadian Girl who Felt God's Call to the Lisu People of China* (Minneapolis: Bethany House Publishers, 1987), 15.
4. Kuhn, *By Searching*, 67.
5. Isobel Kuhn, *In the Arena* (Singapore: OMF International, 1995), 37.
6. Kuhn, *In the Arena*, 47.
7. Ibid.
8. Kuhn, *By Searching*, 47.

DAY 9 — DAVID BRAINERD

1. Edwards, preface.
2. Ibid., April 20, 1742 entry.
3. Ibid., September 20, 1747 entry.
4. Ibid., June 8, 1742 entry.
5. Ibid., June 7, 1742 entry.

DAY 10 — JIM ELLIOT

1. Elisabeth Elliot, *The Shadow of the Almighty: The Life and Testament of Jim Elliot* (San Francisco: Harper Collins, 1958), 132.
2. Ibid., 144–147.
3. Elisabeth Elliot, *Through Gates of Splendor* (Wheaton, IL: Tyndale House, 1981), 20.
4. Jim Elliot, *The Journals of Jim Elliot,* ed. Elisabeth Elliot (Grand Rapids, MI: Fleming H. Revell, 1978), 18.
5. Ibid., 83.
6. Ibid., 172–174. The quote comes from Jim's entry on October 28, 1949. On October 24, he wrote, "I sense the value of good Christian biography tonight, as I have been reading Brainerd's Diary much today." Elliot mentions Brainerd's diary again on October 27.

DAY 11 — SARAH HALL BOARDMAN JUDSON

1. Arabella W. Stuart, *Lives of the Three Mrs. Judsons: Mrs. Ann H. Judson, Mrs. Sarah B. Judson, Mrs. Emily C. Judson, Missionaries to Burmah* (Boston: Lee and Shephard Publishers, 1855), 113–114.
2. Ibid., 111.
3. Emily C. Judson, *Memoir of Sarah B. Judson: Member of the American Mission to Burmah* (New York: L. Colby and Company, 1848), 21–22.
4. Ibid., 112–113.
5. Ibid., 113.
6. Ibid., 125.
7. Edward Judson, *The Life of Adoniram Judson*, 374. Just after George Boardman passed away, Adoniram Judson reported, "One of the brightest luminaries of Burmah is extinguished; dear brother Boardman has gone to his eternal rest. I have heard no particulars, except that he died on returning from his last expedition to the Karen villages, within one day's march of Tavoy. He fell gloriously at the head of his troops, in the arms of victory; thirty-eight wild Karens having been brought into the camp of King Jesus since the beginning of the year, besides the thirty-two that were brought in during the two preceding years."
8. Stuart, 152.
9. Judson, *The Life of Adoniram Judson*, 376.
10. Adoniram Judson, the leader of their mission team, anticipated that Sarah would stay in Burma to continue the work among the Karens. He wrote to her soon after Boardman's death, saying, "I think, from what I know of your mind, that you will not desert the post, but remain to carry on the work you have so gloriously began. The Karens of Tavoy regard you as their spiritual mother; and the dying prayers of your beloved are waiting to be answered in blessings on your instructions." Ibid., 382–383.
11. Stuart, 173.

DAY 12 — ELISABETH ELLIOT

1. Stuart, 166.
2. Ibid., 167.
3. Elisabeth Elliot, *The Savage, My Kinsman* (Ann Arbor, MI: Servant Books, 1981), 9.
4. Ibid., 13.
5. Ibid., 13–14. Elliot quoted 1 John 2:17.
6. Elliot, *The Shadow of the Almighty*, 9.
7. Elliot, *The Savage, My Kinsman*, 14.
8. Stuart, 166.
9. Rose, 47, 143; Elliot, *The Savage, My Kinsman*, 24–25, 28.
10. Elliot, *The Savage, My Kinsman*, 22.
11. Ibid., 25.
12. Ibid., 28–29.
13. Ibid., 66.
14. Stuart, 122.
15. Rose, 198.
16. Elliot, *The Savage, My Kinsman*, 63.

DAY 13 —ROBERT MORRISON

1. Marshall Broomhall, *Robert Morrison: A Master-Builder* (London: Student Christian Movement, 1927), 39.

DAY 14 — GEORGE MÜLLER

1. Charles Dickens, *Oliver Twist* (Oxford: Oxford University Press, 1966), 12.
2. Arthur T. Pierson, *George Müller of Bristol and His Witness to a Prayer-Hearing God* (London: Flemming H. Revell Company, 1899), 31.
3. George Müller, *The Life of Trust: Being A Narrative of the Lord's Dealings with George Müller* (Boston: Gould & Lincoln, 1873), 111.
4. Pierson, 395–398.
5. Ibid., 398.
6. Müller, *The Life of Trust*, 116. Müller quoted Psalm 81:10.
7. George Müller, *The Autobiography of George Müller* (New Kensington, PA: Whitaker House, 1984), 41–42.
8. Müller, *The Life of Trust*, 463.
9. Dr. and Mrs. Howard Taylor, *Hudson Taylor and The China Inland Mission*, vol. 2: The Growth of a Work of God (Littleton, CO: OMF International, 1995), 42.
10. Dr. and Mrs. Howard Taylor, *Hudson Taylor and The China Inland Mission*, vol. 1: The Growth of a Soul (Littleton, CO: OMF International, 1995), 400.
11. Taylor, *Hudson Taylor and The China Inland Mission*, vol. 2, 182–183.
12. Müller, *The Autobiography of George Müller*, 130–131.
13. Ibid., 155.

DAY 15 — WILLIAM CAREY

1. S. Pearce Carey, *William Carey* (London: Carey Press, 1934), 28.
2. Ibid., 36.
3. Ibid., 47.
4. Ibid., 34–36, 48.
5. Ibid., 49–50.
6. Ibid., 75–78.
7. The poet William Cowper in his hymn, "Jesus, Where'er Thy People Meet," also referenced Isaiah 54, and some have thought William Carey's sermon may have inspired this verse: "Behold, at Thy commanding word. / We stretch the curtain and the cord; / Come Thou, and fill this wider space, / And bless us with a large increase." Ibid., 75.

DAY 16 — PATRICK OF IRELAND

1. St. Patrick. *The Confession of St. Patrick*. Public Domain. Patrick was a Celtic Christian who lived before the Roman Catholic church took its current form. The Roman Catholic Church later began considering Patrick to be a saint, but his beliefs differed from those now held by the Roman Catholic Church. The Roman Catholic doctrine and tradition of canonizing saints did not even begin until hundreds of years after Patrick's death.
2. Ibid. Patrick quoted Matthew 28:19–20 and Mark 16:15.
3. Ibid.
4. Ibid. Patrick quoted Psalm 55:22.
5. Attributed to Patrick of Ireland, St. Patrick's Breastplate, translated by Kuno Meyer. Padraic Colum, ed., *Anthology of Irish Verse* (New York: Boni and Liveright, 1922), 111.

DAY 17 — WILLIAM TYNDALE

1. William Tyndale, *Doctrinal Treatises and Introductions to Different Portions of the Holy Scriptures*, ed. by Henry Walter (Cambridge: The University Press, 1848), 135.
2. John Foxe, *Actes and Monuments of These Latter and Perillous Dayes* (London: John Day, 1563), 570. The original spelling is "If God spare my lyfe ere many yeares, I wyl cause a boye that dryveth the plough, shall knowe more of the scripture then thou doest."
3. Tyndale, 135.
4. Robert Demaus, *William Tyndale: A Biography* (London: The Religious Tract Society, 1886), 348. Tyndale quoted Acts 27:34.
5. Tyndale, 137.

DAY 18 — STANLEY DALE

1. Don Richardson, *Lords of the Earth: An Incredible but True Story from the Stone-Age Hell of Papua's Jungle.* (Glendale, CA: Regal Books, 1977), 164. Dale quoted Matthew 28:19–20 and 16:18.
2. Ibid., 351.

DAY 19 — EDWARD JUDSON

1. Quoted by Delavan L. Pierson, ed., *The Missionary Review of the World*, vol. 40 (New York: The Missionary Review Publishing Company, 1917), 933.
2. Judson, *The Life of Adoniram Judson*, 455.
3. Ibid., preface.
4. Ibid., 20.
5. Quoted by Delavan L. Pierson, ed., *The Missionary Review of the World*, vol. 40, 933. This quote, often attributed to Adoniram Judson, was actually said by his son. Perhaps Edward repeated what he had heard his father say before him.

DAY 20 — ERIC LIDDELL

1. Catherine Swift, *Eric Liddell* (Minneapolis, MN: Bethany House Publishers, 1990), 173.
2. David C. McCasland, *Eric Liddell: Pure Gold: The Olympic Champion Who Inspired Chariots of Fire* (Grand Rapids, MI: Discovery House, 2001), 248.
3. Eric Liddell, *The Disciplines of the Christian Life* (London: Society for Promoting Christian Knowledge, 1985), 27–29. Liddell referred to Zechariah 4:6.
4. Ibid., 78.
5. Ibid., 27.
6. Ibid., 29.
7. Ibid., 30.

DAY 21 — AMY CARMICHAEL

1. Elisabeth Elliot, *A Chance to Die*, 63.
2. Ibid., 99–103.
3. Ibid., 350–351. This author finds the second criteria, "the Word of the Spirit in our heart," to be vague. Carmichael could merely be referring to the Holy Spirit

bringing Scripture to mind in a certain situation or during the process of making a decision. Alternatively, the phrase could be interpreted as direct revelation from God. However, if she meant hearing "thus saith the Lord" when she spoke of "the Word of the Spirit in our heart," it would seem there would be no need for the other two criteria. As this author observes Carmichael's amazing life of dedication to God, he notes that at times Carmichael seems to have employed rather mystical means or Scripture taken out of context to determine God's will. This chapter attempts to encourage the reader to catch her passion for following God's will without necessarily endorsing all her methods.

4. Ibid., 211.
5. Ibid., 223.

DAY 22 — MARY SLESSOR

1. W. P. Livingstone, *Mary Slessor of Calabar: Pioneer Missionary* (New York: George H. Doran Co., 1917), 115.
2. Ibid., 175
3. Ibid., 173–174.
4. Ibid., 301.
5. Ibid., 112.
6. Ibid., 19.
7. Ibid., 32.
8. Ibid., 52.
9. Ibid., 55.
10. Ibid., 129. Slessor referred to Daniel 3.
11. Ibid., 143.
12. Ibid., 162.
13. Ibid., 163.
14. Ibid., 179.
15. Ibid., 194.
16. Ibid., 196.
17. Ibid., 212.
18. Ibid., 299.
19. Ibid., 309.
20. Ibid., 312.
21. Ibid., 310. Slessor alluded to Revelation 4:10.

DAY 23 — JOHN MCCARTHY

1. Dr. & Mrs. Howard Taylor, *Hudson Taylor and the China Inland Mission: The Growth of a Work of God*, 168.
2. Ibid., 169.
3. Ibid., 173–177. McCarthy referred to Romans 6:4–6 and quoted Galatians 2:20.
4. A short biography of Taylor by his daughter-in-law, Mrs. Howard Taylor, bears this title.
5. Taylor, *Hudson Taylor and the China Inland Mission: The Growth of a Work of God*, 175.
6. "'He was a joyous man now,' added Mr. Judd [a coworker in the China Inland Mission], 'a bright, happy Christian. He had been a toiling, burdened one before,

with latterly not much rest of soul. It was resting in Jesus now, and letting Him do the work—which makes all the difference! Whenever he spoke in meetings, after that, a new power seemed to flow from him, and in the practical things of life a new peace possessed him. Troubles did not worry him as before. He cast everything on God in a new way, and gave more time to prayer. Instead of working late at night, he began to go to bed earlier, rising at five in the morning to give two hours before the work of the day began to Bible study and prayer. Thus his own soul was fed, and from him flowed the living water to others.'" Ibid., 173.

7. Ibid.

8. Another fellow missionary, C. T. Fishe, wrote, "His [Hudson Taylor's] favourite theme in those days was the fifteenth chapter of John. We had many helpful times of prayer and study. He seemed to be growing much in spiritual things, and that passage was his special delight." Ibid., 181.

9. Hudson Taylor, *China's Millions*, vol. 1 (London: Morgan & Scott), 41.

10. Ibid., 315.

11. Ibid., 607.

12. Norman Grubb, *C. T. Studd: Athlete and Pioneer* (Atlantic City, NJ: Worldwide Revival Prayer Movement, 1943), 43.

DAY 24 — STEPHEN METCALF

1. Ronald Clements, *In Japan the Crickets Cry: How Could Steve Metcalf Forgive the Japanese?* (Oxford: Monarch Books, 2010), 53.

2. Steve Metcalf's biography claims he once beat Eric Liddell in a race, but other biographies of Liddell dispute this claim. According to biographer Duncan Hamilton, Liddell's only defeat not in a relay race came just a few months before his death as he suffered with the effects of what they later discovered to be a brain tumor.

3. Clements, *In Japan the Crickets Cry*, 53.

4. Ibid.

5. Ibid.

DAY 25 — JOHN ELIOT

1. Nehemiah Adams, *The Life of John Eliot: An Account of the Early Missionary Efforts among the Indians of New England* (Boston: Massachusetts Sabbath School Society, 1847), 9.

2. Ibid., 55.

3. Ibid., 78–79.

4. Ibid., 244.

5. Ibid., 245–247. Prominent pastor Cotton Mather wrote of the spread of Christianity among the Native American population in New England and the training of their men for ministry: "The number of preachers to the Indians increases apace. At Martha's Vineyard, the old Mr. Mayhew and several of his sons, or grandsons, have done very worthily for the souls of the Indians; there were fifteen years ago by computation about fifteen hundred souls of their ministry, upon that one island. In Connecticut, the holy and acute Mr. Fitch has made noble essays towards the conversion of the Indians. . . . And godly Mr. Pierson has, if I mistake not, deserved well in that colony upon the same account. In Massachusetts we see at this day the pious Mr. Gookin, the gracious Mr. Peter Thacher, the well accomplished and industrious Mr. Grindal Rawson, all of them hard at work, to turn [them] . . . from darkness to light, and from Satan unto God. In Plymouth we have the most active

Mr. Samuel Treat laying out himself to save this generation, and there is one Mr. Tupper, who uses his laudable endeavours for the instruction of them."
5. Yes, the Native American leader had a very European name. Before the war, this Wampanoag chief, also called Metacomet, requested that the colonial settlers in Plymouth give him an English name. King Philip's father had negotiated peace treaties with the pilgrims and presumably, Philip wanted to continue the good relationship. That all changed with the war.
6. Ibid., 274.

DAY 26 — GEORGE WHITEFIELD

1. George Whitefield, *George Whitefield's Journals* (Lafayette, IN: Sovereign Grace Publishers, 2000), 307.
2. Ibid., 163.
3. Arnold A. Dallimore, *George Whitefield: God's Anointed Servant in the Great Revival of the Eighteenth Century* (Wheaton, IL: Crossway, 1990), 47.
4. Ibid., 134–135.
5. Ibid., 135.
6. Ibid., 138.
7. Ibid., 66. A similar quotation, "The world is my parish," is attributed to John Wesley, reflecting Whitefield's and Wesley's shared perspective on the scope of their gospel ministries. Wesley's quotation is engraved below his statue near Wesley Chapel in London.
8. John Charles Ryle, *A Sketch of the Life and Labors of George Whitefield* (New York: Anson D. F. Randolf, 1854), 27–28.

DAY 27 — HENRY MARTYN

1. George Smith, *Henry Martyn: Saint and Scholar, First Modern Missionary to the Mohammedans* (London: The Religious Tract Society, 1892), 466–467.
2. Ibid., 224.
3. Ibid., 213.
4. Martyn's father was converted under the ministries of Wesley and Whitefield. Martyn himself read Whitefield's sermons.
5. Ibid., 240.
6. Ibid.
7. Ibid., 203–204.
8. Ibid., 150.
9. Ibid., 442. Martyn referred to Philippians 1:20.
10. Ibid., 459.

DAY 28 — WILLIAM BORDEN

1. Mrs. Howard Taylor, *Borden of Yale '09: The Life that Counts* (Philadelphia: China Inland Mission, 1957), 106.
2. Ibid., 209.
3. Ibid., 211.
4. Ibid., 218.
5. Grubb., 170.
6. Taylor, *Borden of Yale '09*, 211.
7. Ibid., 260.

DAY 29 — DAVID LIVINGSTONE

1. William Garden Blaikie, *The Personal Life of David Livingstone Chiefly from his Unpublished Journals and Correspondence in the Possession of His Family* (London: John Murray, Albemarle Street, 1881), 67–68.
2. Ibid., 34.
3. Ibid., 125.
4. Ibid., 41–42.
5. Ibid., 226.
6. Mrs. Howard Taylor, *Hudson Taylor's Spiritual Secret* (Singapore: OMF International, 1932), 18. The quotation is exactly the same, word for word.

DAY 30 — NICHOLAS LUDWIG VON ZINZENDORF

1. Rev. August Gottlieb Spangenberg, *The Life of Nicholas Lewis Count Zinzendorf* (London: Samuel Holdsworth, 1838), 5.
2. Ibid., 15.
3. Jennie Chappell, *Women Who Have Worked and Won: The Life-Story of Mrs. Spurgeon, Mrs. Booth-Tucker, F. R. Havergal and Ramabai* (London: S. W. Partridge, 1930), 107. This book does not specifically identify the painting. However, since the location and inscription are the same, the painting is assumed to be the same.
4. *Report of the First International Convention of the Student Volunteer Movement for Foreign Missions* (Boston: T. O. Metcalf & Co., 1891), 12.
5. The author of this book is a descendant of the Moravians of Germany, Pennsylvania, and North Carolina.
6. Levin Theodore Reichel, *The Early History of the Church of the United Brethren* (Nazareth, PA: Moravian Historical Society, 1888), 116–117.
7. Charles H. Robinson, *History of Christian Missions* (New York: Scribners, 1915), 50.
8. A. J. Lewis, *Zinzendorf, the Ecumenical Pioneer: A Study in the Moravian Contribution to Christian Mission and Unity* (London: Westminster Press, 1962), 92.

DAY 31 — ALL THINGS NEW

1. Smith, *Henry Martyn*, 184.
2. Livingstone, *Mary Slessor of Calabar*, 261.
3. Ibid., 337.
4. Judson, *The Life of Adoniram Judson*, 152.
5. Richardson, *Lords of the Earth*, 352.
6. Smith, *Henry Martyn*, 452.
7. Ibid., 513.

ACKNOWLEDGMENTS

I would like to thank God who saved me and put me into the ministry. Only because of Jesus Christ and His death and resurrection do I have hope for today and for eternity. I rest on His promise of salvation by grace through faith.

I would like to thank my wife, Ellie, for her encouragement to write this book. Without her, this devotional would not exist. Ellie was my first and most frequent beta reader. She was the sounding board throughout the process, a patient ear to an obsessive husband.

Thank you, beta readers! Some of you were kind of biased— like my dad, Steve Conrad, who gave helpful suggestions anyway. Thank you, Micah Colbert, for your exuberance and your frequent messages encouraging me to get this book published and marketed to those who will benefit most. Thank you, Deborah Lake, for doubling as a beta reader and the first editor. Thank you, Andy Overly, for your attention to detail and for catching when my tone was not what it ought to be. Thank you, Mark Vowels, for giving me confidence that the book was worth the effort to publish. Thank you, Matt Herbster, for expressing how the testimonies in the devotional moved you and for providing insight into how younger readers might respond to the truths in the book. Thank you, Tim Leaman, for your expertise in church and missions history. Thank you, Jonathan Johnson, for your ideas on how to improve the visual aspects of the book. Every beta reader made valuable contributions. Thank you all!

I would also like to thank those who polished the book to its final form. Thank you, Ivan Mesa, Joe Tyrpak, and Chris Anderson, for your editorial work. You spotlighted the rough sections and helped me improve my writing. Thank you, Erik Peterson, for designing such an attractive cover and interior layout that reflects the message of the book so well. Thank you again, Joe Tyrpak, for your diligent attention to detail in the final typesetting. Finally, thank you, Church Works Media, for publishing this book.

To God be the glory. May He use this book to further His work throughout the world.

SCRIPTURE INDEX

Made in the USA
Columbia, SC
25 March 2021

35047335R00117